LE CHON

C000042393

NEW CENTURY, NEW SOCIETY

Edited by Dermot A. Lane

New Century, New Society

CHRISTIAN PERSPECTIVES

the columba press

First published in 1999 by

the columba press

55A Spruce Avenue, Stillorgan Industrial Park, Blackrock, Co Dublin

Cover by Bill Bolger
Origination by The Columba Press
Printed in Ireland by Colour Books Ltd, Dublin.

ISBN 1 85607 272 X

Contents

Introduction

Dermot A. Lane

It would be unfortunate if the celebration of the millennium in Ireland became an occasion for Christians to look back triumphantly over the last 2000 years. To be sure there is much to celebrate and to be thankful for in regard to the Christian reality. But equally, however, we know that the history of Christianity has been a mixture of success and failure, sin and grace, light and darkness. Commentators often distinguish between the living reality of Jesus and Christianity as embodied institutionally in different ecclesial communities. It is the mystery of Jesus as the Christ, the incarnation of the Word and Wisdom of God in history, crucified and risen, and present in the Spirit in the churches and the world, that is the proper object of celebration and thanksgiving at the end of 2000 years. The failure of the churches to embody and manifest adequately the face of Christ to the world is a matter of concern to all Christians. The end of the second millennium is an unique opportunity for Christians of all shades to engage in a process of soul searching, repentance and conversion so that in the third millennium the liberating and compassionate face of Christ may be more visible in church and world.

This collection of essays brings together a series of searching reflections on the quality of life in Ireland at the end of the twentieth century. The purpose of the papers is to offer as it were 'an audit' or 'a snapshot' of what is happening in Ireland on the eve of the new millennium. Key areas of life have been chosen for review with particular aspects addressed by individual contributors. Other areas could have been chosen. To this extent the audit initiated is incomplete and the snapshot only partial.

Each author was invited to describe, from his or her particular perspective, the changes and developments taking place in Ireland in the 1990s. In the context of the existing social and cultural realities obtaining in Ireland, contributors were asked to offer a critical evaluation of these realities from a Christian perspective. It is hoped this volume will initiate a mutually critical correlation between the contemporary Irish situation and the Christian message. It is possible that out of this conversation some of the challenges facing Ireland in the new millennium might begin to emerge.

The context of these reflections is twofold: Ireland on the threshold of a new millennium and the call to celebrate the Jubilee year 2000AD. Mention of the millennium triggers a great variety of reactions: Y2K compliance, commercial opportunism, computer failures, frenetic partying, nostalgia, and optimism about the future. These reactions will take place within a framework of time that is described as a *chronological* sequence. There will be a movement in time from December 1999 to January 2000AD and within that movement the kind of time in question is know as *chronos,* a sequence or continuum of uninterrupted time.

In contrast, there is another kind of time, known as *kairos,* a quality time in which new meaning, new interpretations and a new praxis can burst forth. This kind of time is Jubilee time, a privileged time that interrupts and transforms the tedium of *chronos* into *kairos. Kairos* can be a time of disturbing grace, a moment of examination about individual and corporate identity, and a painful confrontation with the truth about existence and history.

Jubilee time for the Jews and for Jesus was described in terms of bringing good news to the poor, a possibility of release for captives, the recovery of sight for the blind, and freedom for the oppressed. Jesus in his preaching described this privileged time as a time in which the blind can see, the deaf hear, the lame walk and the dead are raised up. To reduce the words of Jesus to the physical only is to miss a major aspect of his preaching. Frequently, Jesus complains about those who have eyes but do not see and those who have ears but do not hear. This complaint of Jesus remains as pertinent today as it did 2000 years ago.

The challenges that faced Israel in the fifth century BCE and Jesus in 30AD are strikingly similar to the challenges facing Ireland in the celebration of Jubilee in the year 2000AD: bringing good news to the poor, sight to the blind, hearing for the deaf, freedom for the oppressed, the cancellation of debts, respect for the land and care of the environment. Through the ministry of Jesus the fulfilment of these challenges gained a foothold in history; in virtue of his death, resurrection and outpouring of the Spirit, the church was summoned to continue the ministry of Jesus by addressing these and similar challenges in the world.

The articles contained in this collection outline some of the challenges facing society and the churches in Ireland on the threshold of a new millennium. The challenges articulated are varied and complex; they cannot be easily summarised. At best only a flavour of what is found in the different essays can be sketched

Andrew Pierce opens the reflections by looking at the current vogue in spirituality alongside the existence of a serious theological deficit in church and society. Bruce Arnold analyses the impact of the information explosion on politics. He fears that the relation between the media and politicians is in danger of becoming a spectator sport for the public. Tom Giblin offers a reflection on the causes of Ireland's current prosperity and a critical assessment of its implications. Anne Looney looks at some of the tensions within the current discourse on education, and proposes a re-visioning of education for the future. Sean McDonagh argues that the most important issue facing humanity is the continual degradation of the planet earth and seeks a response to this from the gospel of Christ. Mary Sutton reviews Ireland's performance in its relations with the developing world. She suggests that our positive self-image as empathetic and generous can be challenged on a variety of fronts. Garret FitzGerald traces the dramatic changes in Irish demography of the past forty years. He notes the radical change in *mores* after 1980 and instances how over half of first pregnancies have become non-marital. John Horgan identifies and analyses a number of enemies of the truth, both external and internal to the media. Gerry O'Hanlon challenges the churches to develop an adequate theology and practice of reconciliation, with particular questions about Roman Catholic eucharistic theology and practice. Denis Carroll asks is it possible for the churches to address a problem of which they have been a part and is it the case that politics reflects our unspoken 'values'? Aidan Mathews recalls a devotion from a dying church to see how the one that is being born might find a new way. Michael Drumm shows how ritual and worship have been thrown into question by contemporary consciousness. In response to this question, he outlines the possible significance of religious celebration for our times. Linda Hogan considers the intricate nature of the relationship between women, men and power. She suggest we are still struggling to comprehend the complexities of power and the way it infuses all our relationships and institutions. Patrick Hannon notes a shift in debate from questions about church and state to politics and religion. He suggests that self-righteousness is not a good starting point for finding better ways in the future. Dermot A. Lane concludes the volume by examining the state of Christian faith at the end of the twentieth century and outlines the possible shape of faith for the twenty-first century.

In highlighting these challenges the question arises: will the movement from 1999 to 2000AD be one of mere *chronos,* that is, a continuation of the same, empty time, or will it be a liberating and transformative time, that is, a *kairos* that makes a difference to church and society, refusing a repetition of past mistakes, and holding out new hope for the future?

Christianity – A Credible Presence?

Andrew Pierce

The presence of Christianity in Ireland has been – and remains – so widespread and multifaceted that its very ubiquity seems almost to preclude calling the credibility of this presence into question. The philosophical and ideological criticisms of religion in general, and of Christianity in particular, which have developed in the modern period – that is, since the eighteenth century – have impacted only minimally on Irish Christianity.

So it may be useful to begin by enquiring into what is calling the credibility of Christianity in contemporary Ireland into question. In many ways this is a difficult question to raise, let alone answer, because of what might be termed the theological deficit in Irish society. Elsewhere in the Western world, Christian theology has had to respond to and engage with various forms of reflective atheism. In Ireland, however, the case against Christianity is rarely articulated explicitly as an intellectual argument, and so the challenges to the credibility of Christianity may make their presence felt in a more subtle fashion.

Irish Christianity in transition

As the twentieth century draws to a close, Irish Christianity, despite its large number of adherents, is in a state of transition. In the early and middle decades of the century, the Irish churches enjoyed considerable social power and prestige. In recent decades – and especially since the late 1980s – there have been dramatic changes. At the heart of this transition is a move on the part of the churches from being widely unchallenged authorities, to being seen as institutions which are open to question, and whose views may be ignored. The contrast between the Ireland which listened to Archbishop McQuaid and the Ireland which watches 'Father Ted' indicates the extent to which public perception of the churches has altered over a comparatively short period of time. In the Ireland of Father Ted, religious professionals are represented, no longer by intelligent and socially influential figures, but by an all-male threesome consisting of a conman, an idiot and a reprobate.

This is not to suggest that Christianity has simply moved from being a locus of power to being the focus for ridicule: that is much too simplistic. A certain sense of street credibility is accorded to a number of distinctively

Christian contributions to public debate: for example, the analysis and critiques of the 'Celtic Tiger' made by the Justice Office of the Conference Of Religious of Ireland (CORI), or in the work of the Evangelical Contribution on Northern Ireland (ECONI) which seeks to reflect critically on the identity of evangelical Protestantism in Northern Ireland. Whilst the reputation of these groups – and others like them – resists the easy ridiculing of Christianity, it is evident that these contributions presuppose the credibility and value of a Christian presence in Ireland.

So where do we find the credibility of the Christian presence called into question? Irish Christianity makes its presence felt ecclesiastically, much more so than philosophically or ideologically. It is a noticeable feature of the transitional situation of Irish Christianity that it has given rise to a questioning, not of Christianity *per se*, but of the churches and their behaviour. An absolute separation between Christian credibility and ecclesiastical behaviour – between theory and practice – is contrived, but a distinction between the two is important. To limit the discussion of Christian credibility to the churches and their performances involves an exclusive concentration on practice, to the neglect of theory. This presents a genuine and unusual difficulty for those who wish to raise philosophical or theological questions concerning Christian credibility, or who wish to commend the significance of the claims made by the Christian tradition. It is important, therefore, to explore the ways in which criticisms of the churches may impact on – or may fail to make their mark on – the discussion of Christian credibility.

The deeds (and especially the misdeeds) of the churches will invariably impact on the credibility of Christian witness in Irish society. This is especially the case given that the prevailing philosophy of popular culture seems to be largely constituted by a cocktail of pragmatism and positivism. This is not to play down the significance of protests against ecclesiastical injustice: they cause scandal – both to those directly involved and to those who are compromised in less direct involvement. Nonetheless, it is important to acknowledge that these protests against the churches' actions and/or inactions do not necessarily call into question the coherence or credibility of Christianity as a worldview.

It would not be difficult to draw up a list of those areas where Irish churches have, by their actions or inactions, provoked conscientious protest. Within the past decade alone, church authorities have faced, and continue to undergo, severe scrutiny for their inept response to the victims and perpetrators of child abuse, or for collusion in the social mechanisms of sectarian division – and the list could be extended. It is significant, however, that many of these protests are concerned with seeing justice done in and by the churches. Indeed, if these protests come from within the churches, they may be articulated (explicitly or otherwise) on the basis of Christian theological concerns with justice, equality and inclusiveness. Rather than constituting a challenge to the credibility of Christianity, the criticism and questioning of the churches presupposes a fundamental hope in the capacity of the churches to rectify scandalous behaviour.

A new interest in spirituality

In addition to signs of protest, there are other aspects of Irish ecclesiastical life which are widely understood as signs of vitality within the churches. Perhaps the most dramatic of these is the recent upsurge of interest in spirituality. But is this widespread concern with 'spirituality' necessarily a sign of vitality in the churches? And is it necessarily – as it is sometimes presented – indicative of just how credible Christianity is?

A detailed engagement with the various forms of spirituality being practiced in contemporary Ireland would be a major and fascinating undertaking, but it lies beyond the concerns of this essay. It may be useful to consider a number of characteristics of this trend, perhaps the most obvious of which is that it is flourishing. Prayer groups, meditation, retreats – sometimes run by parishes or dioceses, sometimes organised outside the ecclesiastical mainstream, sometimes even blurring the differences between religious traditions – are omnipresent in Ireland.

The extent to which spirituality is market-friendly will be confirmed by even a quick browse through major bookshops or through the catalogues of religious publishers. Moreover, this craving for matters spiritual evidences a disparity between the popularity of spirituality and the popularity of works of theology or religious studies. Religion is selling, critical reflection on religion remains significantly less popular.

Popularity, of course, does not rob the recent interest in 'spirituality' of value or significance, but it should oblige us to investigate critically the issues raised by this popularity. A number of recent works of spirituality have been concerned with connecting spirituality and justice, and with correcting the bias against affectivity found in much Western religious thought. These are welcome developments, but not every aspect of the vogue for spirituality is as critically aware as these.

Spirituality is a slippery term to define, but in the history of the Christian churches, spirituality – or spiritual theology – was regarded as an intrinsic element of participation within a religious tradition: it was the lived experience of that religious tradition. Rather than attend simply to what spirituality is, or is assumed to be, it is perhaps more important to pay attention to that against which spirituality is popularly defined. It is common to find, whether explicitly stated or assumed, that spirituality is an entirely separate enterprise from either religion or theology. Indeed, to adapt George Orwell's phrase, it is not unusual to meet with supporters of the slogan 'Religion (or theology, or church) bad, spirituality good'. In other words, spirituality, in its more marketable forms, has moved from being an important element within a religious tradition, to practically supplanting that wider dimension of the tradition, including its theology.

A further issue which merits attention is the extent to which the literature of spiritual consumerism is directed towards the modern individual. The relationship between modern individualism and Christianity raises a number of fundamentally significant questions. For our purposes the basic question is concerned with the extent to which Christian believing and belonging can part company, and yet retain a distinctively Christian identity. It is not necessary to subscribe to some form of ecclesial collectivism in order to insist that social imagery in the Christian tradition (e.g. 'body', 'congregation', 'people,' 'church', etc.) possesses more than decorative value. Part of this issue is concerned with the way in which hope – a central theme in the Christian tradition – is inescapably linked with social institutions. The Christian faith has never existed independently of institutional expression and, however imperfect these institutions may have been or may become, to reject institutionality *per se* is, in the final analysis, a refusal of hope.

In Christianity, playing off the spiritual against the social has a long, and not entirely reassuring history. It does, however, connect with a suspicion of social institutions which is part of a wider cultural climate of opinion. In his recent book, *Clashing Symbols,* Michael Paul Gallagher includes the injunction, 'Thou shalt not trust institutions' as one of the ten commandments of radical post-modernity. Whilst not everyone in Ireland who finds contemporary forms of spirituality congenial can safely be described as a radical post-modernist, the overlap between a cultural ethos which is suspicious of institutions, and the popularity of spiritualities which treat social institutions as optional, is certainly striking. 'The distinctive marks of Christianity stem not from the social but from the spiritual side of our lives', according to Mrs Margaret Thatcher's address to the General Assembly of the Church of Scotland in 1988. It is odd, to say the least, to see the socio-spiritual legacy of Thatcherism being served up once more, albeit this time with a devotional flourish.

From a theological standpoint, there is an odd sense of *déjà vu* about all this. The appeal to interiority and individualism in some of the spirituality available in our day exhibits some of the traits of late nineteenth, and early twentieth century theology – traits which have undergone severe scrutiny in the meantime. This insight, which theology provides, is important, because one of the characteristic features of popular writings on spirituality is their

appeal to the past, usually to a past and a tradition which extends consider-
ably further back than one century.

The terms 'mysticism' and 'religious experience', for example, appear regularly – sometimes interchangeably – in both popular religious and secular
discourse ('Mystic Meg' is about as secular as it gets). Yet the antiquity we
may ascribe to the meaning of these terms is open to question. The first,
'mysticism' as a noun, is a fairly new kid on the linguistic block, having
appeared only in the modern period in seventeenth century France.
According to leading commentators on the history of mysticism, after the
nineteenth century, 'mysticism' had acquired a new meaning, which was
focused on a specific type of experience, which a limited range of people (the
mystics) 'had'.

As far as I have been able to ascertain, the characteristically modern usage
of the term 'religious experience,' to refer to discrete instances of bizarre
experience, was first promoted by William James in his classic work, *The
Varieties of Religious Experience,* which was published in 1902. For James,
'religious experiences' bypass traditions and institutions (such as churches or
language) and involve the catapulting of an individual into direct contact
with God. This way of understanding 'religious experience' has proven highly
influential – it has found its way into everyday language as the apparently
'obvious' meaning of the term, and it has also found a home in the scholarly
literature of both theology and the philosophy of religion.

Even though James' views have become widespread, his thesis has been
subjected to extensive criticism, most of which has focused on his belief that
religious experience is essentially a matter of direct, immediate encounter
between God and an individual human being. Recent writers have tended to
lay greater emphasis on the complicated dynamics of all human experience,
including religious experience and mysticism. Contemporary theology
emphasises the formative role in religious experience played by – to take a
number of inter-connected examples – language, tradition, gender and
embodiment.

There is, therefore, a curious overlap between ideas and assumptions
which philosophers and theologians have tested and found wanting, but
which remain eminently market-friendly. It would hardly help the case for
Christian credibility if many Irish Christians were choosing to interact devo-
tionally with an historically dubious past, rather than reflecting – in penit-
ence and hope – on our more recent past and its heritage. It is precisely the
lack of this critical examination of Christianity – theoretical and practical –
which was referred to at the start of this paper as the theological deficit in
Irish society.

A theological deficit in Irish society

This lack of space, for a critical and self-critical examination of Christianity in its Irish context, has impoverished both public debate and the life of the Irish churches. In particular, we have been noticeably lacking a theology of culture, that is, a sustained attempt to bring contemporary culture and the insights of the Christian tradition into dialogue with one another.

Part of the blame here lies with the way in which theology has been taught. In recent decades there has been a significant change, but for most of the twentieth century, theologically-literate circles were of the small and ever-decreasing variety, made up for the most part of those who were being prepared, or who were preparing others, for ordained ministry. Irish theology, therefore, has tended to be seen as a church-based activity, operating according to the agendas of the churches, rather than as an intellectual discipline with a wider audience in Irish society.

The significant change has been the growth in interest shown by lay-people, and especially women, in theology. It is important to note that this is not simply a change in audience – volunteers replacing conscripts – which leaves the subject-matter unaffected. Rather this change of audience is provoking changes in how theology is taught and what kind of theology is taught.

Perhaps the most famous definition of theology was provided by Anselm, a monk who became Archbishop of Canterbury in 1093, who described theology as 'faith seeking to understand itself'. Since Anselm's day, however, theology has become increasingly conscious that its task involves more than explicating the contents of the Christian faith, the truth of which can be assumed. It also involves taking into account the various philosophical and ideological challenges to the credibility of this faith which have been proposed.

Thus for most of the past century, the kind of theology widely studied was unlikely to foster strong links with the emergent culture of modern Ireland, but instead saw itself as being primarily responsible to the interests of the various churches. This has, in part, contributed to a suspicion that theology is insufficiently distanced from the churches and may not, therefore, be a suitable subject for study at third level. Out of responsibility to the rest of the scholarly community, it is important that theologians resist this suspicion. The distinguished American theologian, David Tracy, has pointedly observed that religion 'is the single subject about which many intellectuals can feel free to be ignorant.' This kind of ignorance minimises the scope for engagement between Christian faith and culture in contemporary Ireland, and it is a contributory factor to the Irish theological deficit. It is thus all the more important to highlight the critical character of theology; theology is not a matter of intellectual public relations for the churches. It is an intellectual discipline, which, like other disciplines, seeks to reflect – critically and self-critically – on its subject matter, in this case, the Christian faith.

This paper has discussed the ways in which the presence of Christianity in Ireland may have its credibility questioned. Attempts to isolate and consider a limited number of features in the current transitional state of Irish Christianity are bound to be partial. Nonetheless, the features considered here – debate and criticism of the churches' behaviour, and the burgeoning spirituality industry – are features which are acknowledged at a popular level to be characteristic of our situation.

I have suggested that these features are symptomatic of a culture which lacks a sense of the possible value of theological input to the life of the churches and to wider public debate. The way in which the cataloguing of ecclesiastical misbehaviour so easily supplants the discussion of Christian credibility, is in the interests of neither that discussion nor of the churches' attempts to engage with criticism. Spirituality, despite its evident attraction, may, in some of its less critical manifestations, resemble an ideological Trojan horse, filled with baptised, but uncritiqued assumptions shaped by modern individualism and consumerism.

These points confirm the need to address the theological deficit in Irish society. In particular, the Irish situation requires a theology which will operate at a critical distance from religious faith, and which will shape its critical perspective in dialogue with the diverse cultural concerns of contemporary Ireland. Serious engagement between faith and culture requires theology to work on the boundaries between the two. And, as Paul Tillich – one of this century's finest theologians of culture – never tired of pointing out, 'on the boundaries' is the ideal location for truly creative theology.

Politics, Information and Democracy

Bruce Arnold

The eucharist, as an expression of Christian faith, contains certain affirmations of belief which are common to the two main churches on this island. They include love of God and love of one's neighbour. There is the symbolic re-enactment of the Last Supper, and the expression of the belief that we consume the Body and Blood of Christ, and do so in remembrance of him. The service is often accompanied by the giving of 'the sign of peace', which is also symbolic of a collective consent and agreement in this, the most common of all the sacraments. And though past centuries have been notable for argument and conflict over the differences between the Mass and the Communion Service, the modern tendency is to focus on the similarities and points of agreement.

For those in communion with their churches, the idea of common ground is more real than the arguments over transubstantiation. Unfortunately, the numbers who now agree are only a tiny fraction of those who disagreed in times gone by. And the very idea of Christian morality as a force in the modern world is an increasingly faint aspiration. Yet this reinforces the verities for those who do believe, and draws them together, out of potential disagreement and into a common bond.

The force of Christian morality is increasingly faint within the narrow confines of politics. Why this should be so is a massive question, involving all sorts of social and historic changes. It remains a constitutional imperative, reinforced by law. But the period in Irish life when it occupied a central position in the life of the country, and was backed by huge church authority in the state's affairs, has gone, and is irrecoverable. No bad thing, many would say. And this is true in terms of the authoritarian nature of the regime, the exclusivity over the interpretation of faith, and the distorting effect this had on people's lives. But it should not embrace the abandonment of the spiritual life altogether, nor will it; and it should not exclude altogether the place of that spiritual dimension within the public political life of the people. We may have abandoned the special position which the Constitution once gave to the Roman Catholic Church, as the church of the majority; but we have not yet abandoned the forceful Christian sentiments with which the Constitution is presented in its preamble, nor have we expunged the statement about power deriving from God, contained in Article 6.

I propose to consider the changed circumstances in which faith has to be seen in the context of public and political life, and to do so in two areas of critical importance, trying to relate them back to the issue of morality, and then of Christian morality.

The first concerns the extent of information, and how this affects public involvement in, and judgment of, the political process. The second concerns the nature of democracy and how we are to preserve it during the coming century.

The information explosion

The preservation of democracy is a key issue for the future. So too is public involvement in the political process. And the two are closely related. They are also closely related to the information explosion, which now, to a very large extent, governs our lives. The populations in the countries of the developed world are under perpetual bombardment with information. On what is almost a daily basis, this is refined and extended. The way information comes to us, and how it is steadily being improved, is an industry itself, servicing the technology. And both are highly profitable while at the same time being complex and confusing. The information explosion itself concerns domestic politics, international politics, war, culture, social affairs, sport, entertainment, pornography, commercial trade, finance, investment, collecting, dating, hobbies, gossip, even just chat. All brands and types are frenetically pursued on the internet, competed for between television channels and among radio channels, competed for even between programmes in the same channels, and delivered every morning of our lives in daily newspapers and other publications which are fatter and more cumbersome than they have ever been before.

We are flooded by information to an extent that has changed the imperative about who seeks whom. There was a time when the onus was on the individual to seek to inform himself about what was going on, to set his or her own limitations on the extent of what the individual needed to know. Now the imperative is the opposite: the individual increasingly has to find ways of excluding the vast bulk of what is on offer, in order to make sense of what matters. Our privacy from the information invasion is more difficult to obtain than the information itself.

The information, moreover, has become an end in itself. T. S. Eliot once asked the important two-part question: 'Where is the wisdom we have lost in knowledge? Where is the knowledge we have lost in information?' That was in 1934, in his poem, *The Rock*. He could not have envisaged just how massive the changes would become, before the end of the century, and how overwhelming a force information, as an end in itself, would become.

Journalism and politics are intimately bound up in the processes which surround the gathering of information, and its analysis and dissemination. And the two forces are often in conflict. Within the period during which I have been professionally engaged in finding out what politicians say and do, and what it means, there has been a huge revolution. In the early 1960s reporting on political life was narrow and restrictive; analysis, particularly where it involved criticism and confrontation, was a singularly rare activity. Authority was of paramount importance. Respect for office, and for the holders of office, was a starting point. And to many of those who exercised power, the role of the media was that of a conduit through which the public would be informed of intentions and decisions. These, along with their speeches, would be reported. And the arena of conflict or confrontation would be the Oireachtas. It was sober in its operation. And though coverage was in the form of a summary of verbatim reports, the whole approach left the elected members and the ministers in comparative privacy. The writing of colour stories was rare, and a weekly comment-piece was the normal limit.

It remained true, through all of this, that the supposedly important arm of democracy, the press, and radio and television, fulfilled a task. Also, that it was the one designed over centuries to protect freedoms and to expose activities which are an abuse of power. But no one saw how limited it was, and it took two decades of the media working away at this task to bring the fundamental change which confronts us now.

We applaud the evolution of a dynamic, multi-voiced, 24-hour coverage. We welcome the choice of media, from newsprint to internet. We grow familiar with the innumerable men and women working fulltime on the interpretation of what politicians say and do, and on judgments which can be funny, harsh, serious, flippant, well-informed or otherwise, first, second or third-hand.

But the people have changed. They read and follow events with the level of fascination given to good films and novels, or successful soap operas on television. But increasingly, they see no connection with their own lives, or they see it in terms of entertainment and are prepared to take no action other than continuing their support for their chosen newspaper and their interest in their favourite radio and television programmes. There is a growing tendency for the work of the media in exposing misdemeanour, sometimes in hysterical terms, to be seen to have thereby 'done the business'. The mopping up process, which is something handed back to the political institutions, often leaves them puzzled and unable to act.

An obvious example, which has dominated public interest during the last five years of the century, is the series of increasingly controversial tribunals. This method of examination and interrogation, attracting huge public interest when it was applied to the beef industry, and then turned on other areas of possible corruption or dishonesty, has both reinvigorated and immunised public affairs. The reinvigoration derives from the obsessive public interest. The immunisation derives from the fact that so little results from the huge investigation and display of information. What, after all, came out of the Beef Tribunal?

More recently, the press, together with radio and television, have shown prodigious energy in reporting and analysing the work of the more recent tribunals dealing with possible corruption over planning and the payment of money to politicians. It has been a primary focus of attention, eclipsing the Northern Ireland Peace Process, the war in Kosovo, the unprecedented success of the Irish economy, and the impact of this on property prices. We have had the facts. We have had the analysis of the facts. We have had the re-enactment by actors of the various exchanges before the judges, and various figures, including barristers, the judges themselves, and most notably Mr Gogarty, have become part of a modern folklore.

Is it that the information explosion, the right of access to documents, the sustained interrogations conducted by tribunals, Dáil committees, the courts themselves, rendered us morally and politically sterile? Does the public view the apparent duel going on between the politicians and the media as a form of spectator sport in which the people have no role except that of audience?

It is hard not to form this conclusion. Opinion polls and election results suggest as much. So do the performances of our leading politicians. People in public life show an increasing ability to excuse themselves on every question raised about what they knew and what they did about their knowledge. And this seems also to confirm this curious form of moral sterilisation.

What we, that is the people, do about it is more than just an electoral matter; or at least, it should be. If a moral vacuum is being created, and the contest between the media and politics turned into a spectator sport, then action to rectify the dilemma falls back on the public's shoulders. And how they deal with this seems to be one of the crucial issues for the coming century.

Democracy and information
Justifying this argument, which is one in favour of greater individual action in the field of politics, is by no means easy. What, after all, are political parties for? The information explosion, in my view, has largely detached political activity from moral constraint. And it has undermined the principles of consent and involvement which are essential to the working of democracy. Democracy is not a spectator sport. Democracy is not the exercise, periodically, of a vote in an election. Democracy is, or should be, the government of the people, by the people, all the time. It may work through intermediaries, the elected representatives, and those they appoint to run the Executive. But

it is not something to be handed over to the media to exercise on behalf of the people. And this is the present tendency.

It is a tendency aided and abetted by the concept and practice of political clientalism. And this is particularly reinforced by the political system in Ireland which depends on proportional representation in multi-seat constituencies. Politicians are conditioned by this machinery to compete with each other in the performance, often of menial, demeaning and at times dishonest tasks on behalf of voters. Clientalism is based on the idea of patron and client. It is as ancient as the art of politics itself. At its worst, it involves money buying favours, or political support buying favours, and it runs counter to all the fundamental principles of democracy as we should know them.

All political parties, by the nature of the game, are obliged to offer some kind of return to their supporters. Democracy wouldn't work without this Yet it really does not work with it, either, since clientalism is at odds with the democratic principles of egalitarianism and fairness.

The political party makes multifarious offers which are often deliberately ill-defined in some areas, generalised in others, specific in very few. They range from ideologies and principles, on the one hand, to jobs, contracts and planning permissions on the other. The style and nature of the response to the demands of clientalism are usually dependent on what your politics are.

For various reasons, during the past three decades, Fianna Fáil has been associated with the non-ideological end of this list of principles, rather than with the policy-based and more generalised view of some kind of national benefit. Various tribunals have identified how members of the largest party worked the system to the benefit of supporters, and why this in turn supposedly worked to the benefit of the party. And to a large extent the architect of this change was Charles Haughey. He created a political culture, and it became a legacy. Whether, in reality, it worked at all, except to make some people richer than others, is open to question. Unlike his predecessors, he failed repeatedly to turn the kind of clientalism in which he appears to have indulged to any real electoral advantage, thus frustrating his own attempts to increase his political power. But he did establish a new image for Fianna Fáil, the dark side of which has been so elaborately exposed by the very information explosion inimical to his and the party' aims.

The party is still linked to that culture in a number of different ways. Now that the whole country knows how it works, where it worked, what kind of figures were involved, who operated the system best, and what a huge nonsense much of it was anyway, what has been the result?

The answer is: very little. Clearly, from election results in 1997 and in 1999 – arguably, in the European and local elections, the last of the decade – while Fianna Fáil did not increase their support, and had the misfortune of losing a seat to Dana in the European elections, thus reducing their representation, they still recorded solid backing for what they represent.

This means that the denial of democracy is strongly evident within the very process by which democracy is sustained. We have a belief in the party system which is based on an expectation that supporting a particular party can bring benefits, and some people deliberately want those benefits to be unfair. This belief is widely held through the social spectrum. Wealthy interests believe that supporting a particular party will lead to advancement. The poor believe that support for a different party will lead to their improvement at the expense of the wealthy. And within individual constituencies, people believe that their support can be correlated to benefits sought and obtained by the elected member on behalf of his constituents.

Very few believe that clientalism and democracy are mutually incompatible, and that a properly-run democratic state should not require the political intermediary in order for the citizen to obtain his justified rights. Nor is there necessarily a better way, achieved by removing the competitive practices which derive from the multi-seat constituency as compared with a proportional representation system of election for single-seat constituencies. The level of clientalism in the British political system is clear evidence, both at the highest levels, where major contributions by wealthy individuals then result in privilege or preference, and at lower levels, that electoral reform is no guarantee of the better working of democracy.

Democracy is something for which legislation is only part of the answer. A fundamental requirement is also that of consent. The governed consent to be governed. The parties out of power consent to the system which sets them in opposition, doing a legitimately recognised job of interrogation and criticism. The parties in power consent to the inevitability of their removal and replacement, by the will of the people. They are temporary guardians. Democracy demands their consent to this.

Out of the principle of consent emerges, or should emerge, the practice of consensus. Modern international politics is uniquely an expression of this. At no previous stage in history has there been such widespread agreement about the requirements of modern democratic states. The harmonisation of European law and practice, the international agreements which govern trade and tariffs, the concept of the world being collectively policed, collectively saved from starvation, and in due course, either collectively or nation by nation, being led towards the consensus of democracy, is not too far-fetched, and is in marked contrast with the attitudes held internationally in our lifetimes, which tolerated dictatorship, totalitarianism, and other forms of tyranny.

These changes are not upon us yet. But the process leading towards them, greatly enhanced by the information explosion – one of its benefits – would seem to be irreversible. In principle, we have seen the expression of it over Kosovo, a collective desire to be good, humanitarian world policemen. It is a selective urge, not applied to South America, Africa, the Middle East, the Far East. In practice, the urge and its forcible expression in warfare has brought the West and the international community into a state close to chaos before roughly righting itself. In all probability it has created a sterile problem-state, not unlike Bosnia. And as with Bosnia, judging that is a matter for the long-term future, well into the century we now approach.

The hugely enhanced, modern-day information process, keeping us better informed about more activities, domestic and international, than ever before, imposes an importance on events vastly in excess of their real relevance. The old historical principle on which countries formulated their policies, particularly foreign policy, used to be self-interest. This has been engulfed and replaced by a much wider principle of humanitarian concern, world justice, and a belief in the superiority of democracy.

In Ireland, journalists, while they are not necessarily disposed to moral positions, are nevertheless conditioned to be suspicious of any form of politics which depends upon a patron-client relationship. By a process of elimination, they side with democracy and express various forms of the belief in fairness and equality which is fundamental to the law and Constitution of the country.

In this, without being necessarily moral, or necessarily Christian, they approach more closely to the ideals of Christian belief as expressed in acts of worship such as the eucharist. Unfortunately, they are consistently unable to impose the standards which emerge, sometimes implicitly, sometimes explicitly, from their reports and judgments. Politicians suffer the examination, bear the criticism, and go on as before.

In this there seems no role for the public beyond the exercise of electoral mandates from time to time. For the rest, they are a vast audience for the non-stop political game played out in the media.

If, in the next century, there is to be a greater integration of all the participants in the political process – reporters, commentators, political activists, audience – then it must come from the greater exercise by ordinary people of their democratic rights and responsibilities. Quite how this is to be achieved is, in my judgment, a supremely important millennium problem. The politicians and the media have to concede more power and encourage their greater exercise within the third partner in democracy, ordinary people. The vote on its own is not enough.

The Irish Economy:
Wondering about Wealth

Tom Giblin

Ireland is surfing into the new millennium on the crest of a wave of unpreced-ented economic success. During the last six years of the old millennium the output of our economy (GNP) has grown at over 6% each year and unem-ployment has fallen rapidly to below 100,000. The long despaired-of objective of full employment is actually within sight. With government coffers flush and the national debt reduced to manageable proportions, the focus of econ-omic government has changed dramatically, from the fiscal imperative to save money of the 1980s, to the task of how to spend a burgeoning fiscal surplus wisely.

Of course there are disconcerting eddies in the wave that threaten to knock us off balance, such as the gaps in housing and infrastructure. We face these problems, however, with resources in hand to construct a solution. It would be churlish not to applaud our dramatic change in fortunes; a change that has caused us as much surprise as joy.

In what follows, first we track the journey of our economy over the past few decades, trying to trace the causes of our current success. In the second part of the chapter we reflect from a Christian perspective on our funda-mental attitude towards our prosperity and the free market economy that has delivered it. We also examine some important limitations to our progress such as the persistence of inequality and increasing degradation of the envir-onment. Finally, in a third section, we explore the relationship between our new wealth and the cultivation of fundamental inter-subjective goods such as trust, community, love, respect, etc.

I. THE ECONOMIC JOURNEY

A half-full glass begins to overflow?

The depth of our surprise at our recent economic success is, I think, the product of the sharp contrast in our economic fortunes that stretches back over the post war period. At the mid 1980s when Kieran Kennedy, Deidre McHugh and I were writing about the record of Ireland's economy this cent-ury, we concluded that the performance of the economy could only be described as mediocre. The economy, however, was significantly better adapted structurally to develop in the future than it had been in the past. We remarked then that our mediocre performance would appear better if future progress showed that these structural changes had created a solid basis for progress. By 1986, however, little evidence of this had yet emerged. The national debt and unemployment were both at their historic peak.

Looking back then, it seemed that the shadow of the grim decade of the 1950s had stretched over an equally grim decade, the 1980s. Of course the causes behind the economic failure in each decade were quite different, yet one key consequence, the massive inability to provide adequate employment for our population, was the same. By contrast, the period of growth of the 1960s into the early 1970s, when we had full employment and limited emigration, appeared to be exceptional.

A retrospective on the eve of the new millennium gives a quite different picture to that possible in 1986. In the prosperous 1990s the period 1960-1975 no longer looks exceptional. Instead it is the 1980s that now appear aberrant. The success in both prosperous periods was built on policy changes, forged in the depths of the failure of the preceding decade, that, when combined with a set of favourable external circumstances, led to real economic progress. Moreover it is only in the 1990s that the development strategy of the 1960s has been confirmed as capable of delivering prosperity on a par with our European neighbours.

Success wrought out of failure
During the 1950s Irish society took the often-analysed step of changing from a protectionist inward-looking economic strategy towards an export-oriented outward-looking strategy. The failure of that decade was the key stimulus to this major policy change. The Irish economy had been dependent on exporting one product with slow growth in demand (food) to a slowly growing market (the UK). The inward-looking policy of setting up protected industries to serve the home market failed because these enterprises never had sufficient scale to become internationally competitive. Thus there was no strongly growing sector to employ those leaving agriculture, nor the large numbers of young people entering the labour force. The landmark policy changes in the 1950s are familiar, from the establishment of the IDA in 1952, to T. K.Whitaker's report, *Economic Development,* in 1958.

In the 1980s the causes of the crisis were different. Once again, however, a key policy choice was a crucial factor so the sense of having failed to manage our own affairs was equally real. A rapid expansion of the public service and a large scale programme of public infrastructure spending in the late 1970s inflated both wage expectations and government borrowing. The spending spree left us vulnerable when, after the second oil price shock in 1979, Western governments responded by raising real interest rates. Our national debt began to grow out of control. The prolonged recession in the UK after 1980 also rocked our economy, lowering the demand for exports particularly from indigenous Irish industry.

It took a decade of fiscal prudence to overcome the problem of the national debt. From 1981-1986, public capital spending was reduced sharply and taxes were increased substantially. This, however, depressed demand on the home market, which in turn hit many indigenous Irish companies struggling at the same time with high real interest rates and deep recession in the UK. Unemployment soared, hitting tax revenues and increasing social welfare payments. The national debt continued to rise. From 1987 onwards our situation began to ease. This time current government spending was curtailed along with capital spending cuts. At the same time the UK economy began to boom. Irish industry exporting to the UK became more competitive as sterling appreciated. The country was also significantly helped by the doubling of EU Structural Funds which financed increased capital projects after 1989.

More buoyant tax revenues meant that the government could embark on a new approach to pay agreements that exchanged real wage restraint for tax cuts. Social partnership developed out of the crisis and has been one important foundation of the current boom. The partnership agreements have delivered a stable and more competitive wage context, as against the conflictual industrial relations of the 1970s and early 1980s. They have also been a forum for policy change in which the social partners have taken responsibility for the general interest rather than adopting an exclusively sectional approach. Future partnership agreements should be an appropriate context for sharing out the fruits of our success. Key issues need to be faced, however, such as delivering tax cuts for the low paid, balancing private and public sector wage growth, profit sharing and managing wage increases in a way that maintains our competitiveness.

Like the outward turn in the 1950s, fiscal prudence and social partnership have both been important lessons learnt out of failure.

Other roots of success

The bedrock of the 1990s boom is our open export-oriented economy. We have benefited in particular from multinational companies producing here for export. US foreign direct investment in Ireland has increased from

$14,400 (per Irish manufacturing worker) in 1983 to $30,000 in 1996. Of course this increase is linked to policies such as low manufacturing tax rates, education of the workforce, and the expertise of the IDA. There is more than policy at work however. Ireland has also proved attractive because it is in the European Single Market and is English speaking.

During the 1980s there was much criticism of our reliance on foreign direct investment. It was argued that these companies had poor links with the rest of the economy. The difficult situation for Irish companies also under-lined our dependency, as did occasional big foreign company closures that rocked different areas. These criticisms are less often heard now, however. Foreign companies operating here are now more deeply linked into the econ-omy, spending much more here than they did before. Foreign owned manu-facturing jobs also last longer on average than indigenous manufacturing jobs. Also Irish export oriented industry has become more successful and has benefited from the presence of the multinationals in areas such as software development.

Apart from manufacturing success, the economy has also reaped the divid-end from education. Ireland is ranked second in the OECD for the propor-tion of the 25-34 age group that have third level qualifications. However, it only ranks 14th for the proportion of the 25-64 age group that have third level qualifications. Younger Irish people are very well educated but the older generations are less well so. This situation will obviously improve over time. Our educated workforce, especially in areas where there are global skill short-ages, has been an attraction for companies to come here. It has also helped increase research and development in our industry and also spillover of know-how from multinationals to indigenous companies.

A final important factor has been the demographic dividend. Ireland was unusual in the 1980s when compared to other EU countries in having a very large number of young and old people relative to those of working age. This has changed during the 1990s as larger younger generations entered the workforce replaced by smaller generations of young people behind. When combined with growing employment, more women working outside the home, emigrants returning, and the unemployed getting jobs, this means that the overall numbers depending on those in jobs has fallen sharply from over two towards one and a half. Clearly this has the potential to bring benefits to all.

The outcome produced by the combination of these policy changes and factors not so much of our own making, has been a remarkable convergence in our GNP per capita towards the European average. The chart below illus-trates the dramatic nature of this convergence.

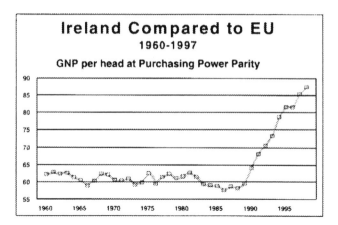

Source: ESRI, *National Investment Priorities for the Period 2000-2006,* p. 32.

II. PERSPECTIVES ON PROSPERITY

On the border of the promised land

From a Judeo-Christian point of view it is interesting to examine our attitude to our recent economic history. A relevant scriptural reference is the narrative context of the Book of Deuteronomy which is set dramatically (not historically) on the border of the Promised Land. The people ask what frame of meaning (torah/teaching) will they have 'to replace' the basic teaching 'obey the law and you will arrive in the Promised land' that sustained them as they wandered in the desert. Now that they are about to enter the Promised Land the old frame of reference is no longer so strongly operative. After all, they are in possession of the Promised Land, so why still worship and obey God?

The analogy between the desert time and our crisis decades, and entry into the Promised Land and our recent prosperity, is suggestive. More pertinent again are the two fundamentally differing attitudes to prosperity traced in Deuteronomy, chapter 8. The first one forgets what has been given and says 'my own strength and the might of my own hand won this for me'; wealth itself becomes the object of worship. The other attitude remembers the reality of history, the journey into prosperity and the help received along the way when the people were poor and vulnerable. This attitude is marked with gratitude that leads to generosity, while the other is characterised by greed and selfishness. The tension between these two attitudes is also visible in Ireland at the edge of a new millennium.

Our new found national wealth is the work of our hands but not entirely so. It has, in part, been given to us by the EU, the foreign multinationals, the benefits of our location and language, positive economic contexts in the US and UK economies, etc. Therefore, we should not grasp it selfishly as if we had earned it by ourselves alone. Our prosperity is also a somewhat tarnished gift since we benefit disproportionately from the world economic order while other countries are significantly excluded or disadvantaged. Ethically, then, we cannot absolve ourselves of responsibility for the disadvantaged in our world and in our country. In this light it is significant that during the 1990s while we gave nearly £650m in official development assistance we would have given £2.25 billion (both at 1995 constant prices) had we fulfilled the UN target level of development assistance of 0.7% of GNP to which we are committed. Being one of the richest countries in the world brings its own responsibilities from a Christian point of view.

The recent controversy about refugees and asylum seekers in Ireland also shows two attitudes in conflict. Some argue that we have earned our own wealth by ourselves and should not have to share it with foreigners. Perhaps they are concerned with issues of cultural integration. However, more fundamentally, they forget that we were integrated elsewhere. Others remember our story of emigration and the opportunities our people were given. The ethical imperative of this history is that we too in our turn should be generous in welcoming others and providing opportunities for them. Yet movement in this direction to date has been somewhat grudging.

The corrupt acquisitiveness of tax evasion, planning favours, and political kickbacks, so amply exposed in recent times, also expose a set of attitudes to wealth and prosperity that are marked more by greed than by generosity.

Perhaps the most dramatic example of tax evasion is outlined in the 1999 Report of the Comptroller and Auditor General into the deposit interest retention tax (DIRT). It documents the extent of the use of bogus non-resident accounts to avoid tax. A memorandum, from the Department of Finance's files on the 1993 Tax Amnesty, suggested that about half of non-resident accounts (then containing £4bn) may have been fraudulently designated, for the purpose of avoiding tax, by depositors who were in fact resident. The sheer number of accounts and the length of time the abuses were tolerated before decisive action was taken, shows that tax evasion was not just confined to a small elite in Irish society.

It can be surmised that at root many in Irish society have an ambivalent attitude to paying taxes. They regard the money they earn as theirs alone and only have a weak sense that taxation pays for services that they and their children benefit directly from, not to mention a sense that ethically they should pay tax to help those who have been less fortunate than themselves.

Of course, formerly high levels of taxation, an excessive burden of taxation on income as opposed to property, and recent indications of tax evasion by the wealthy and powerful, have not helped foster a positive attitude to paying tax.

Taxation, however, is not the only area in which we have a culture of possessive individualism (or perhaps more accurately 'possessive familialism' – 'everything for my family regardless of anyone else'). It is also deeply ingrained in our attitude towards, and legal protection of, the rights of private property. Our Supreme Court, for example, has been very reluctant to effectively temper the claims of private property by constitutional provisions on equality, social justice and the common good. Similar issues are also at stake in our dysfunctional compensation culture with its extraordinarily high levels of frequency and compensation of minor claims.

These possessive attitudes about tax, private property and compensation have their roots in our traditional attachment to the land, our post-colonial ambivalence towards the state and the law, right wing ideology that assumes the state will waste taxpayers' money, and also simple greed. Alongside such attitudes, however, there is also evidence of traditional generosity in Ireland. Yet the recent fall in charitable giving and in charitable volunteering indicate perhaps a less generous Ireland to come.

To return to Deuteronomy, the proper Christian attitude on the border of the Promised Land is not 'my own might and the strength of my own hand' have won my propery and wealth for me; instead it is gratitude and generosity because this good fortune is as much gift as achievement. Possessive attitudes are not compatible with the Christian belief in the universal destination of goods. Life, the earth and our wealth most fundamentally are given to us. Therefore they are never simply ours to do with what we please.

Providence and the market

Another area for consideration from a Christian standpoint is our attitude towards the free market. At one level the market is simply an historically and socio-culturally conditioned way for people to express their preferences, acquire goods, and sell the produce of their labour. This is both useful and necessary. It is also clear that to develop our economy we simply had to produce and sell our wares on world markets. This fact contrasts with a common reflex in some Christian circles to think of 'the market' as a negative thing.

At one extreme, arguing that markets are bad *per se*, I suggest, is a bit like King Canute who stood on the beach and ordered the tide not to come in to prove his omnipotence. He got wet! The view is strong on critique but weak on alternatives to the market mechanism. This is not to say that markets are not in need of criticism. They most certainly are. More precision is needed, however, if we are to distinguish those cases where we need to deepen and widen markets from those where we need to be wary of their influence.

One prejudice against the market is that it is associated with greed. The fact that freeing up markets can be egalitarian, however, is often overlooked. Increased competition in air transport, for instance, has facilitated the boom in Irish tourism. Introducing competition into the telecommunications industry has lowered prices and attracted the telesales industry. Both these industries provide employment for a wide range of workers including the lower skilled. There are other areas that might also afford wider opportunities for Irish people if they were opened up to increased competition. Waiting for a taxi in Dublin 'drives home' the point!

The British theologian, John Milbank, however, points to a danger that arises from the very benefits of markets. He argues that belief in the 'invisible hand' of the market as described by Adam Smith often can become theological when it replaces belief in Providence. Market benefits can seduce us into an overestimation (divinisation) of their capacity to deliver the goods necessary for full human life, leading to another extreme and equally flawed view, i.e. that markets are good *per se*. While markets should be extended in some areas, we should also be aware of their intrinsic limits.

The market can be understood as a game with rules. One limit in the market game is that it relies on competition and motivates participants through external or monetary incentives rather than internalised virtue. The focus of competition is on getting things done, problem solving, advancing towards the goal of attaining the scarce good. Yet the key weakness of market competition is the counter side of its strength. By motivating people and organisations through rewarding the highest achievers most, it affords them increased monetary strength to achieve other goals. The competitive market tends to pick winners and make them stronger – inequality of outcome. Also since people approach the market with radically different buying power it is not a level playing field – inequality of participation. Thus some goods (e.g. healthcare, housing) have, at least partially, to be taken out of the market.

A roof over your head?
In Ireland today the playing field is certainly very unequal when it comes to the housing market. People of different income levels have quite unequal chances to participate in this market. Soaring house prices and rents are eating into the non-housing income of people. In 1997 the share of take-home

income spent on housing by a married couple with no children, earning one and a half times the average industrial wage, was 38%. One can easily imagine the huge share of incomes being spent on housing by those at or below the average industrial wage, especially if they do have children. These pressures have undoubted social consequences. Young couples are taking on a huge burden of debt that often makes a double income and borrowing from parents imperative. Many families no longer have the option of one parent staying at home even when children are very young. In a situation where childcare provision is so inadequate in supply and expensive one worries about the impact of this on the next generation as well as the pressures put on the relationship of the couple themselves.

A promised land for all?
In any game, there is also a problem if the same people always win – inequality of outcome. A feature of our prosperous market economy is that the gap between the winners and the less well off is growing. In this respect the story, told above, of economic success built on open markets, is radically incomplete. It ignores the issue of distribution. Many in Ireland today would laugh at the idea that they are surfing into the new millennium on the crest of a wave. They feel rather that they are drowning in the economic backwash.

It is surely the distinguishing mark of what it is to be Christian (inspired by Matthew 25, 'insofar as you did it to one of these you did it to me') to reach out to those who are excluded. Yet some economists criticise Christian commentators for 'focusing entirely' on the question of distribution and ignoring the issue of wealth creation. Clearly wealth creation should not be ignored because of the opportunities it creates. Indeed the business economy, including the market, private property and free human creativity, is affirmed in the papal encyclical *Centesimus Annus,* paragraph 42. It is a qualified affirmation, however. Markets should not deny economic, religious and ethical freedom broadly understood, and inequality undermines economic freedom.

We live in a three tier society. ESRI figures for 1994 show that the top tier contains 20% of Irish society. They obtain about 44% of total disposable household income. This tier contains people who work in areas such as computing, finance, company owners, senior management, shareholders, professionals, high skilled workers whose skills are in scarce supply, owners of pubs, restaurants and building land, and large farmers. Typically they work hard and relatively are very well rewarded; they are economically in control of their lives.

The middle tier, or 40% of Ireland's people, receives 40% of the disposable income. This tier contains people who work as white collar workers in offices, public servants, teachers, nurses, gardaí, tradespersons, small scale self employed, etc. They have economic concerns about overtime, bonus payments and promotion. They also worry about house affordability and their capacity to repay mortgages. Other concerns might be whether they can change their car, or can they afford childcare if both parents are working, or will their children get the points they need to go to college?

The bottom tier, also 40% of our people, gets only 16% of disposable income. This group contains lower paid workers of all descriptions, those in casual employment, those who are unemployed, single parents, elderly people. It also includes more particularly disadvantaged groups, those with a physical or mental disability, early school leavers, the homeless, those with drug and alcohol problems, refugees and travellers. Life in the bottom tier is economically stressful with concerns like getting into debt, paying electricity, gas and telephone bills, finding money for birthday gifts or a holiday away or occasionally even for basics.

Recent research in Ireland shows that absolute poverty continues to decrease. The poor are not getting absolutely poorer. More people can afford a telephone, a car, central heating, etc., than did a decade ago. On the other hand, relative poverty, where people are badly off compared to most other people, has been increasing over the period between 1994 and 1997. The main reason for the increase in relative poverty is that social security payments have not kept pace with the growth in average income over this period. Also low pay has increased far more slowly than skilled pay. A key policy choice as we face the new millennium is how we can develop the skills of people at the lower end of the labour market and also by how much low pay and social security should increase. If they grow by less than average incomes then those depending on these sources of income will steadily become relatively poorer.

A landflowing with milk and honey or plastic bags and cars?
Another fundamental limit to the power of markets is the range of goods they can organise. In economic parlance, market goods are rival (in other words the more of the good you have the less I have) and excludable (one person owning the good can exclude another from its consumption). Most goods that are scarce in this precise sense can easily and properly be assigned a monetary value in the market place. However, there are so-called public goods that are not fully excludable (radio, security services, roads) and/or not fully rival (knowledge, disease eradication). The free market alone is not capable of providing these goods adequately.

One such category of goods is environmental goods such as clean air, species diversity, clean water, etc. When they are in abundance environmental goods are non-excludable and non-rival. As a result, these goods have no monetary value and the market is blind to them. The only kind of value they have is the value of their existence that we may or may not respect as a value for us. It is only when pollution has destroyed or consumption exhausted these resources, that they become scarce enough to be priced automatically. Many environmental goods are rival in an inter-generational sense. If we consume too much of them now there will be none for people coming after us.

Traditionally our environment here has benefited from a low level of population density and no heavy industry. There are emerging environmental problems, however, as our economy develops.

- The number of private cars on our roads increased by 400,000 between 1987 and 1997. If the level of car ownership in Ireland now pertained planet wide then there would be in excess of 2 billion cars! International agencies predict that there will be 1 billion cars by 2025 and judge that this level is environmentally unsustainable.

- In 1995 Irish households generated 1.8 million tonnes of waste, or over half a tonne per person. The target in the National Sustainable Development Strategy is to reduce this by 20% by 2010. Ninety-two per cent of this waste is landfilled despite the fact that this is the least desirable way of treating it and only 8% is recycled.

- At present forty-one different Irish species (Mammals 2, Birds 32, Fish 6, and amphibians 1) are classified as either extinct, endangered, vulnerable or rare.

It is becoming ever clearer that we need to discourage further growth in car usage. Still most of us think it is our right to own our car and travel in it where we like and when we like, giving little thought to the stress and pollution created by such behaviour when generalised throughout the population. Once again, if we want to meet even our modest target on household waste reduction our behaviour will have to change. This means assessing not just the impact of what we each do individually, but the wider impact when everybody behaves this way. Assuming that I have the right to behave in a certain way in the knowledge that such behaviour is unacceptable or self-defeating if generalised, is effectively claiming a position of privilege with no underlying justification of one's claim.

III. MARKET GOODS AND INTER-SUBJECTIVE GOODS

An Irish camel and the eye of the needle?

There is also another distinct category of goods that the philosopher Alasdair MacIntyre calls 'internal goods'. They are internal to good human practices. These include love, community, respect, trust, knowledge, play, reverence, etc. These 'higher gifts', as St Paul calls them (1 Cor 12:31ff), are inter-subjective goods, not material goods, and free human giving is intrinsic to their production. They are not for sale and are only available within coherent forms of socially establised co-operative human activity in which they are extended and developed.

Internal goods can never be properly expressed in monetary value. Unlike environmental goods, although potentially rival and excludable at the individual level, they become non-rival and non-excludable at the general level. At the individual level, we can't love everybody and we can choose to share our love with some and not with others. Yet at a general level, the more love is present and 'consumed' the more is likely to be 'produced'. A loving community is better at producing caring persons than a heartless one.

The analogy of a game is once again helpful. The internal good is the pleasure and fun of taking part according to what the game requires. The external good is winning a competition and getting the reward associated with it. Winning excludes the rival competitor from the external good. If one is motivated only by the external good, however, then there is no motivation to avoid cheating. On the other hand, if one is motivated by the good internal to the practice, then one must play by the rules. Playing with enjoyment increases the enjoyment of others. The good to be attained is not the competitive good of getting things done, but the co-operative good of being in right relationship.

Aiming for these goods, building the activities within which they are produced, and cultivating the acquired human qualities or virtues that enable persons and societies to realise and extend them, is a profoundly different task from that of the marketplace. It subjugates both the value of getting things done and the value of winning to the value of accepting each person for who they are and relating properly to them.

This approach to life is more basic than the market. For one thing, it applies in contexts where a competitive or market-based approach is meaningless, such as a community of handicapped or unskilled persons. For another, it can be shown to be fundamental to the market economy itself. Francis Fukuyama has explored in depth how the social virtue of trust is essential to economic activity. Without trust contracts would become impossibly detailed, innovation would be regarded as potentially a trick, and arbitration would be rejected as biased. Everything would be referred back to the legal system for resolution, incurring very high economic costs (our compensation culture is a good example). This argument can equally be made about other internal goods such as love, respect, community, even play.

Fukuyama is optimistic that the capitalist system is compatible with the spontaneous sociability of trust that underlies it, though he acknowledges tensions between the individualism behind capitalism and the communitarianism that sustains trust. I think, however, that the gospel warning that it is easier for a camel to get through the eye of a needle than a rich person to get into the kingdom of heaven (Mark 10:26) is less sanguine about the compatibility of wealth and virtue. By extension, I am not so sure of the harmony between the capitalist system of wealth creation and the activities that produce internal goods.

One example of lack of harmony is the tension between a 'vocational' and strictly professional motivation in caring occupations broadly construed to include education, health, child rearing, community development, sport, tourism, etc.. Professional 'care' can be and often is deeply giving. Yet it only becomes so when the professional carer is motivated by the internal good of the activity they are engaged in. The teacher, nurse, child-minder, community development person, sports coach, bed and breakfast proprietor, garda who is exclusively motivated by money will lack something vital. The person being 'cared for' will notice that they are not cared for because of who they are but because of money. In turn that awareness fundamentally undermines some of the internal values at stake, respectively, knowledge, healing, care, community, play, welcome, trust.

This is not to say that professionalisation is necessarily dangerous. It is not. Instead it is to underline that market incentives alone will not cultivate the 'virtues' or human capabilities needed to realise internal goods. These must come from other roots in the culture, be they ethical, religious, or communitarian. Yet the image industry associated with selling is partly corrosive of the cultural roots that sustain internal goods.

Advertising affects the cultivation of virtues in us, through the image of the good life it propagates. It endeavours to make us buy particular products, but has a wider impact. We are stimulated to buy products by their imaged association with a certain ideal of attractiveness, relationship, freedom, pleasure, status, sex, etc. Our lives are imaged for us. As we absorb the advertising and shop, we internalise the proposed images progressively. The more prosperous we are the deeper our engagement will be with the worldview that markets propose.

Yet there is much in such messaging that is inimical to the virtues and activities that are necessary to produce key internal goods. Clearly the image industry tries to convince us that we will be more fulfilled as people if we consume more of the products on sale. It does this by stimulating appetite on several levels: appetite for freedom as absence of constraint, appetite for power and status, appetite for pleasure, appetite for security and insulation from pain. Along with stimulation of appetite comes a promise of satisfaction wrapped in a product.

There are two problems with the promise, however. On the one hand, the product cannot deliver what is promised. Indeed many of the appetites that are stimulated are really only capable of being met (and then frequently not in the exaggerated sense that advertising suggests) in activities that produce internal goods. On the other hand, the market's messages are both individualistic and immediate. It portrays an individual instant notion of happiness. The urgency of the message is of course driven by the need to sell. In effective advertising, however, we are encouraged to imagine that it is the urgency of our need that is at stake rather than this imperative to sell.

This vision of what fulfills the human person, however, is at variance with the patience and practice that are needed to develop those human capabilities of how to love someone, how to trust, play, pray, etc. The image industry cannot deliver these goods because they are not for sale. It also undermines their production, however, by teaching us to compete and consume by investing in activities that feed ourselves now as individuals rather than participate in co-operative activities that really do have the potential to realise these goods.

Perhaps it is not so difficult then to understand why wealth is often an obstacle to appreciation of spiritual values. Nor is it hard to appreciate why the temptation of the people on the border of the Promised Land is to forget things of the spirit and ultimately forget God. The danger of prosperity is that insofar as it undermines the culture, faith, and activities that produce internal goods, it ultimately voids itself of meaning. All it will leave us with is a jaded palate.

It is important to note, however, that the critical interference between the market and the realisation of internal goods is not a radical incompatibility. A dysfunctional economy leading to lack of material goods, unemployment, etc., does nothing to help build love, community, trust, etc. The truth is that each set of goods is needed to better produce the other. The typical error in prosperous times, however, is to believe that market goods will suffice alone.

CONCLUSION

There is much to be grateful for in the prosperity we have achieved. It is the fruit of learning from our mistakes and investing over a long number of years in our economy. Yet it is also a result of good fortune, for we have received much help from others to get to where we are now. We are living in an Ireland in which the modern dream is fulfilled and within this positive context I have tried to trace several challenges.

At the surface lies the challenge to extend the model of success into those areas of inefficiency in our economy. Linked to this extension of opportunity is the more difficult task of building greater social solidarity and reducing inequality. We will not be willing to travel in this direction, however, unless we remember our history in gratitude and avoid lapsing into forgetfulness and selfishness. Our success also throws up more intractable challenges. We face the problem of the unsustainability of our lifestyles. What right have we to degrade the earth's resources and deprive future generations of its enjoyment? What right do we have to consume at a rate that cannot be generalised?

We also face the fact that prosperity re-writes our culture at some depth and poses some dangers for key internal goods that make life worthwhile and underpin social meaning as well as the economy. Inattention to internal goods through excessive attention to consumption weakens a sense of social justice and the common good through its stimulation of and stress upon the private individual. Post-modern fragmentation is not simply the result of an awareness of our fragmented perspective as knowing subjects rooted in a particular history, social place, unconscious and language. It is also provoked by a real fragmentation of human meaning insofar as it is reduced to consumption.

A Christian view of human life argues that internal goods are the most fundamental. The material, rival and excludable goods that the market can deal with are necessary only in moderation. To paraphrase St Ignatius of Loyola, it is not the consumption of many different products that satisfies the desires of the human heart but the interior appreciation and exchange of sufficient external goods and an abundance of internal goods within loving creative human relationships that are open to the transcendent. Amidst the clutter of consumables that prosperity brings, a thirst arises for the simplicity and silence in which we can learn to taste the sacred. Hopefully we will not come to believe we can quench it with a soda!

Select Bibliography

Analysis and data on:

The Irish economy up to 1987:
Kieran A. Kennedy, Thomas Giblin, Deirdre McHugh, *The Economic Development of Ireland in the Twentieth Century,* Routledge, 1988.

The Irish economy in the 1990s:
Frank Barry ed., *Understanding Ireland's Economic Growth,* Macmillan, 1999, in particular Chapters 2,3,4, and 8.

John FitzGerald, Ide Kearney, Edgar Morgenroth and Diarmuid Smith, *National Investment Priorities for the Period 2000-2006,* Policy Research Series 33, ESRI,1999.

Absolute and relative poverty in 1997:
Tim Callan, *et. al., Monitoring Poverty Trends,* The Stationery Office and Combat Poverty Agency, 1999.

The environment:
M. Lehane, ed., *Environment in Focus,* Environmental Protection Agency, 1999.

Housing:
Daithi Downey, *New Realities in Irish Housing: A Study on Housing Affordability and the Economy, Consultancy and Research Unit for the Built Environment,* DIT, 1998.

Non-resident accounts:
Comptroller and Auditor General, *Report of Investigation into the Administration of Deposit Interest Retention Tax and Related Matters during the period 1 January 1986 to 1 December 1998,* July 1999.

Compensation culture:
Bill Toner S.J. and Tony O'Riordan S.J., 'The Claims Industry and the Public Interest', *Working Notes,* Issue 35, Jesuit Centre for Faith and Justice, June 1999.

IBEC, *Personal Injury Compensation as it affects Irish Business, the State and the Public,* Dublin 1999.

Refugee issue:
Bill Toner S.J., 'Wanted: an Immigration Policy', *Working Notes,* Issue 33, Jesuit Centre for Faith and Justice, December 1998.

For underlying philosophical and theological concepts:
Alasdair MacIntyre, *After Virtue: a study in moral theory,* Duckworth, 2nd Edition,1985.

Francis Fukuyama, *Trust: The Social Virtues and the Creation of Prosperity,* Penguin Books, 1996.

John Milbank, *Theology and Social Theory: beyond secular reason,* Blackwell, 1990.

Education for the Next Century: Towards a Re-Vision of Christian Education

Anne Looney

Talking about education ...

Anyone who teaches, or works in, or writes about education is likely to be given a particularly warm welcome these days at parties held in fashionable neighbourhoods, apartments and enclaves by and for the thirty-something generation. Once a teaching 'vocation' has been exposed by the gin and tonic small talk, the guests move in for the kill. I remember how the parties of my twenties were spent defending the long holidays and apparent short hours of teachers. Now, in my thirties, I can spend the entire main course advising on 'good schools' for talented offspring and approaches to getting on the list for the most desirable establishments. I have proved a most disappointing guest, however, by suggesting that eager parents might first consider what sort of education they want for Hannah or Jack, or what sort of education Hannah and Jack might like. Responses range from vague references to 'good' education to more specific requirements to do with hundreds of points, first fifteens and Young Scientist exhibitions!

I have also been at gatherings where the concerns about education and schooling are quite different. How can the uniform be afforded? What about the bus fare? Do families have to provide ingredients for Home Economics? What about the tracksuit for P.E.? Is there bullying in the secondary school? Whatever the context, education, especially when associated with schooling, is always a cause for concern and a focus for debate.

One way in which concern about education is expressed is in precisely these kinds of conversations and questions. Parents want a 'decent' education for their children. They want 'good' schools. And, given the correlations in Ireland between educational achievement and socio-economic success and participation, and between early school leaving and subsequent poverty, such concern is justified.

But the concern about education has a second dimension, focused less on the future life chances of the child but on the future of society as a whole. As one educationalist noted, when society has an itch, schools get scratched.[1]

---

1. Cuban, L. (1990), 'Reforming Again, Again and Again' in *Educational Researcher*, 19 (1), pp. 3-13.

Thus, the solution to every social ill ranging from substance misuse, to the problem of litter, to, most recently, dangerous driving, is to 'cover' it in schools. Such quick fixes are usually proposed by adults who obviously behave exactly as they were taught to in school and who presume that everyone else will do the same! Excellent personal and social education programmes do exist in school but it is naïve to assume that these alone will radically change behaviour.

People are interested in education. Much is expected of education, for individuals and for society. But behind these expectation lie three tensions which, when exposed, might offer challenges and possibilities for those who would wish to re-vision Christian education. And this is a good time for such re-visioning. Because is not a good time for Christian education. And it is a particularly bad time for Catholic education. In Ireland, recent investigations into the approaches to care and education offered by some religious orders have exposed a dark layer of cruelty, brutality and abuse. In the developed world Catholic education is being threatened by the fall in religious vocations and the ensuing disappearance of ordained and consecrated personnel from classrooms and school administration. And in the popular media, Catholic education is presented as something from which one recovers over time, rather than a foundation for a fulfilled and happy life. Recent debates in Ireland about the relationship between religion and education, at the Education Convention for example, in responses to the White Paper and the Education Act (1998), have been largely dominated by the language of power and control as opposed to the language of the gospel or by any specific vision of Christian education. While a debate rages about education and its aims and purposes, it can seem to many that all a Christian vision of education has to offer is the language of control.

An exploration of the three tensions of education might offer the possibility for new words and a new language.

All change or no change? The first tension

Of late, education talk seems to be imbued with urgent overtones. Some would say that such a focus on education is a typical *fin de siècle* trend. Consider the end of the last century, for example, and the development of mass education for all social classes in Britain, and the 1878 intermediate Education Act in Ireland which set the foundation in place for the post-primary system. At the end of the last century too, schools were the focus of considerable attention and considerable pride – in Britain and elsewhere in the Western world. The great Victorian legacy of schools, hospitals and prisons dotted the landscape – social and geographical – as symbols of philanthropic and religious social reform. It is interesting to note that, of these three great social edifices, hospitals have changed a great deal in the last one hundred years, prisons to a lesser extent and schools least of all. The fundamental concept of a teacher in a classroom of students (fewer students than one hundred years ago, admittedly) has changed little in the last one hundred years. The balance of power in schools, based on expert knowledge and the need for socialisation of young people into accepted mores and codes of behaviour, appears to have shifted very little. Students remain largely passive, interaction is based on the verbal cues of the teacher and school life remains an odd throwback to a bygone era. In many Irish schools pupils dress in a uniform which, as students will all too readily point out, owes more to the turn of the last century, than the dawning of the next. Schools, especially post-primary schools, are dotted with weird and wonderful rules about 'bizarre hairstyles', numbers and location of jewellery, length of socks and ties, height of shoes and positioning of shirt collars.

So despite claims of too much change in schools, for many students the school curriculum looks much as it did at the turn of the century and the dynamics of teaching and learning remain driven by the two basic premises that the teacher knows and the student doesn't and that the process of education is about redressing that balance. There are, of course, many innovations which challenge these premises, which promote active and co-operative learning, which see curriculum as created in classrooms rather than delivered by teachers. But such innovations always appear to be found at the peripheries of education, among students who might be at risk of early school leaving, or who are educationally disadvantaged in some way. Or they are found in low stakes contexts like Transition Year (which is not assessed in a state examination). However, in spite of such developments, the core of the teaching process, built on the relationship between the student, the teacher and the skills and knowledge set out in the curriculum, remains resistant to change.

On the cusp of the millennium, in the midst of great social change, the first great tension about education is clear: *Despite considerable change rhetoric, not that much has changed about education for young people in one hundred years.*

The Question of Value: the second tension
The second fundamental tension is the apparent contradiction between what *appears* to be valued in education and what is *really* valued in education. A scan of the national and local newspapers in September, when examination results appear, is a good indicator of this tension. Much coverage is given to the five A student, usually pictured with proud parent or teacher. I have never seen a picture captioned 'average grades, creative, team player, imaginative and independent thinker'. Now it is likely that in the course of the year such

students do feature for their achievements in competitions or projects or for participation in community action – but a clear message is given each September that what is *really* valued is a set of high examination grades, despite the White Paper's assertion that education *seeks to foster a spirit of self-reliance, innovation, initiative and imagination.*[2]

The tension is also highlighted by the comments of a principal of a post-primary school who is alleged to have commented after a lecture on the need to produce students who are independent, critical thinkers, full of imagination and initiative, that she had indeed one such model student in her school … who had been expelled the previous week!! Anecdotal or not, the comment does highlight the tension between what is really valued and what is apparently valued in education. Schools depend for their effective functioning on the passive acceptance of the school regime. Success in exams owes more to knowing the formula for success (hence the proliferation of grind schools) than a display of initiative or imagination.

So far two tensions have been identified – the tension between the unchanging dynamic of the teaching process and the apparent proliferation of educational reform and the tension between what appears to be valued and what is actually valued. The third and final tension arises between education as a future oriented process and a pervasive nostalgia for how things used to be.

Education for the future or for the past? The third tension
Education is a future oriented process and is therefore particularly vulnerable to the millennial rhetoric of bright new tomorrows. Across the globe, countries have been adding '2000' or '21st century' to a whole range of curriculum and educational initiatives – Ireland's Schools IT 2000 project on information and communications technology being a case in point. Former president of the European Commission, Jacques Delors chaired an International Commission on Education for the Twenty-First Century, established by UNESCO in 1993. Its report was published under the title 'Learning: The Treasure Within'. The commission examined the meaning of lifelong learning and challenged the utilitarian view that education is a means to an end. The final report distinguished four 'pillars of learning': learning to know, learning to do, learning to be and learning to live together. Education, concluded the commission, must attend to all four if it is to be truly educational. One of the most striking features of a collection of essays prepared for the commission by UNESCO is that, of its 23 short papers, only two concern themselves with schools. The other 21 focus on learning as a lifelong process and integral part of personal and social development, the key to participation in what is portrayed as the 'learning society'.

2. Government of Ireland (1995) *Charting our Education Future: White paper on Education,* p.10.

The relationship between the education system and the economic system of a country used to be expressed in terms of human capital. Of late this has been replaced with one of the great millennial mantras – knowledge capital. For the information-based society needs not units of labour (as expressed in the human capital theory) but units of knowledge and skills in knowledge creation and application. It's hard to capture what a knowledge society really is. To many adults it is symbolised in changes they never dreamed would come about – an entire encyclopaedia on a disc hardly bigger than a pound coin, a menu of options when you make a phone call, a car that finds its own way, a watch that tells you your precise location on the planet and in the sitting room, an endless supply of television and radio stations. One recently retired executive noted that she had stopped reading the recruitment sections of the national newspapers – a habit of a lifetime – not because she had retired from the job market but because she had found it depressing that she no longer knew what most of the job titles meant and the specifications read as complete mumbo jumbo! The nature of knowledge is changing – as the four pillars identified by the UNESCO commission indicate, *knowing that* is no longer enough. *Knowing how* is needed. Learning to learn has become the indispensable skill for the future. We are already moving from a knowledge society to a learning society.

And yet education and education talk is imbued with nostalgia for how things used to be. While much is made of the role of education in the solution of social and civic ills, there is also a suspicion, voiced by some but held by more, that education may be actually responsible for some of those very ills. Consider the rapid and increasing decline in religious practice for example. Some would point the finger of blame at Religious Education classes in primary and post-primary schools. Students are no longer being taught the basics of their faith, the argument runs, so therefore they lose all interest in it and break any connection they have with institutional religion. This argument is based on two false premises. The first is that Religious Education classes don't deal with the basics of faith – they do. It's just that, like the rules of spelling for example, if students are surrounded and bombarded by a culture imbued with entirely different basics or rules, it is unlikely that those basics will survive beyond the classroom door.

The second false premise is that there is a causal relationship between knowledge and behaviour. Such a relationship assumes that those who smoke know nothing of the risks of cancer because if they did they would stop smoking immediately! Knowledge of faith is only one dimension of commitment. The catechists of early Christianity were well aware of this and emphasised the other dimensions – the role of witness in particular – as well as instruction. More recently, American sociologist Andrew Greely, writing on the particular value of Catholic schools in the United States, singles out two defining features of Catholic education. Writing of the enormously rich and fruitful assets uniquely available to Catholic education, he identifies stronger community ties and 'more imaginative metaphorical resources, particularly as they are expressed in communal liturgy' as its defining features.[3] Not, it is worth noting, the teaching of the 'basics' in Religious Education class.

Such nostalgia of suspicion is not confined to Religious Education. It extends to the full range of school subjects, to manners and attitudes, to crime, to sexuality ... If schools were only doing what they used to do in the past then the future would be more secure!

Further analysis of education talk would unearth many more tensions, but the three explored above offer particular possibilities for those who wish to re-vision Christian education. For Christianity is a faith built on the tensions between past and future, between the real and the apparent and between change and stasis.

Towards a re-visioning

In the light of the three tensions of current education talk, a number of challenges for the re-visioning of Christian education can be identified. However, as has been suggested, a foundational principal of this new vision will be a linguistic one – the language of control must be left firmly in the twentieth century. It will not survive in the twenty-first and the price for continuing to speak it may be high. The education debate will simply move on. And a great opportunity will have been lost.

There are rich sources for a process of re-visioning. Much has been written about Christian education, but perhaps the jubilee celebrated in 2000 might prompt a return to the origins, perhaps even to the words and actions of the founder of Christianity himself. In the ministry of Jesus the language of control was shattered by parable. The concern for, and pride in, institutions and their rules and regulations were constantly challenged by the actions of Jesus which exposed the inequality and injustice of the relationships on which they had been created. Christian churches have produced many documents on education since the time of Jesus. A return to the origins does not require that these be set aside, but looked at anew in the opportunity offered by jubilee and in the light of current education talk.

The first tension – between apparent change and lack of any real change – suggests that the re-visioning process might explore a Christian rationale for educational change. What is effective change from a Christian perspective? Who should benefit from change? How can change be supported and

3. (1998) 'Catholic Schools at the Crossroads: An American Perspective', in J. M. Feheny, *From Ideal to Action: The Inner Nature of the Catholic School Today,* Veritas, Dublin.

made lasting? Many models of educational change exist, most imbued with the language of organisational efficiency and effectiveness. Might the time be right for a model of change for Christian education, imbued with a different language which aims to ensure not simply that change happens, but that good change happens?

The second tension – between what seems to be valued in education and what is really valued – raises fundamental issues for the re-visioning process. For example, how might the re-visioning of Christian education approach the exclusion of a young person from school? Exclusion is a serious matter for any school. But for schools whose ethos includes a fundamental belief in forgiveness or a conviction that no-one is beyond redemption, then a move to expel or exclude a student poses particular problems. The strength of the argument that the educational rights of many well-behaved students is more important that the education of one disruptive student is further challenged by the actions of the founder of Christianity which appeared to value the excluded individual above those who fitted the institutional pattern. The issue is not an easy one, yet 'ethos' is a word used regularly in discussions on Relationships and Sexuality Education but very rarely in discussions on discipline. A re-visioning of Christian education will need to redress the balance.

The third and final tension is between education talk's fondness for the past and the future orientation of the education process itself. This past and future tension is at the heart of Christian faith, and is celebrated in jubilee – 2000 years of faith in the future. A re-visioning of Christian education might look to the vision of the learning society which is emerging in secular re-visioning and see how a pilgrim people might indeed be a model of a learning society – ever searching, ever engaging, ever critical, ever open. It might look at the four pillars of the learning society – learning to know, learning to do, learning to be and learning to live together – and see in them the challenge for all Christians who strive to become what they are called to be.

What is sketched here for the re-visioning of Christian education represents only an initial exploration. But the proposal is born out of a deeply held conviction that such a process is essential. It is essential if Christian education is to feature in the education talk of the next millennium. But it is also essential because education needs its humanising influence. The emerging mantra of the knowledge society – that the truth will make you rich – needs to be tempered by the conviction that real truth will set you free.

The Environment and the Catholic Church

Sean McDonagh

As we face into the new millennium all human beings, and especially religious people, are called to face the fact that our modern industrial society has taken a huge toll on the fabric of life of planet earth during the past one hundred years. We are destroying our air, water, and the life-giving quality sunlight. We are poisoning our soils and causing the extinction of a vast number of creatures which God has placed on this earth with us. Every part of the globe and every ecosystem on earth has been affected. The damage everywhere is grave. In some situations it is irreversible. Unfortunately, church leaders of all traditions, in common with their counterparts in the educational, industrial, political and financial establishment have been slow to understand the magnitude of the destruction.

All that is possible in this essay is to look at how crucial life-systems on our planet have already been damaged and how Christians might respond to this destruction from the well-spring of their own religious tradition.

Land

Poor land management, overgrazing, chemical agriculture, monocropping, deforestation and human population pressures have caused soil erosion and desertification on an unprecedented scale. About 3,500 million hectares, an area the size of North and South America, are affected by desertification. Each year at least another six million hectares are irretrievably lost to desertification, and a further 21 million hectares are so degraded that crop production is severely affected.

Professor David Pimentel and his team at Cornell University in Ithaca, New York, estimates that worldwide about 85 billion tons of soil are lost each year. Most of this damage, unfortunately, is in the Third World where between thirty and forty tonnes per hectare are eroded each year. Even in the US, seventeen tonnes of topsoil per hectare are eroded with each cropping.[1] Top soil is precious; without it no crops will grow and pasture land will not

---

1 . Tim Radford, 'Wearing the World Away', *The Guardian*, March 5, 1995.

be fertile. No machine can readily create topsoil. It builds up slowly and takes between 200 and 1,000 years for 2.5cm of topsoil to build up.

Genetically engineered foods

In recent years many are worried by the developments in genetics and biotechnology that allow genes to be moved between various species that would never interact through normal breeding processes. Today plants and animals with genes taken from completely unrelated species are being engineered in the laboratories of biotechnology companies and released into the environment. Many are worried about the effects of such organisms on human health and on the wider environment.

Even those who accept that a particular genetically engineered crop will not cause human health or environmental damage are worried about the scramble to patent seeds, animals and living organisms which has gathered speed in recent years. They believe that over a short period of time patenting will remove many life forms from the public commons where they have served humans and other creatures for millennia. Under a patenting regime these life forms will become the property of northern transnational corporations. Life will only have value in so far as it generates a profitable return on investment for large companies who, in a decade or so, could control the seed banks for many of the staple foods of the world. The possibility that a small number of multinational companies will control the seeds of the world's staple crops is truly frightening.

In 1998, before the European Parliament voted on the life-patenting directive entitled 'The EU Directive on the Patenting of Biological Inventions', environmental organisations in Ireland, especially VOICE, attempted to ignite a public debate on the issue. Despite the explicit teaching of the Bible that life is a gift from God and that there are limits to human control over life, the churches in Ireland were silent on this issue. It would appear that the pro-life stance is very selective indeed.

Water

Human activity is polluting water in the oceans, rivers, aquifers and lakes. More than 97% of all the water on earth is sea water. During the UNESCO proclaimed International Year of the Ocean in 1998, it emerged that the oceans are being over-fished and polluted at an unprecedented rate. Important areas of the oceans, close to the continental shelf, are contaminated with human, agricultural, industrial and radioactive waste. Much of this is toxic and carcinogenic. Because we have tended to treat the oceans as sewers,

the Baltic, Mediterranean, Black, Caspian, Bering, Yellow and South China
Sea have all been seriously damaged in recent decades. The waters of the Black
Sea, once a flourishing eco-system is now considered to be 90% dead. The
Aral Sea has diminished by one-third and what remains is heavily polluted.

Over-fishing is depleting the oceans and leaving them barren. Many people feel that the oceans are so vast and the variety of fish so abundant that
there would always be vast quantities of fish in the sea. We are now learning
how false those assumptions are. According to a report by the UN Food and
Agricultural Organisation (FAO) in 1995, over 70% of the world's marine
fish stocks are either 'fully-to-heavily' exploited, overexploited, or slowly
recovering.[2]

Only one per cent of the fresh water of the world is available for human
use in either agriculture, industry or for domestic purposes. Access to this
water is very inequitable. World wide the demand for water is doubling every
twenty-one years. Supply cannot keep pace with demand as population soars
and cities explode. The situation in the Middle East and North Africa is precarious. North Easter China, Western and Southern India, Pakistan, much of
South America and countries in Central America like Mexico face water
scarcity.

Water in Ireland
Anyone who lives here knows that Ireland is blessed with a plentiful supply
of rain. Nevertheless the quality of water in many Irish rivers and lakes has
deteriorated in recent decades. Fish kills, unfortunately, still happen each
summer. This is due to the increased levels of phosphorus entering our rivers
from a variety of sources, including sewage treatment plants, factories and
farms. The subsequent algal bloom depletes the supply of oxygen and causes
the fish to die. The CoastWatch report for 1997 complained that the excessive use of nitrate and phosphate fertilisers was polluting Ireland's coast to a
'very worrying' degree.[3]

There is also grave concern about the quality of ground water. A report
from the Environmental Protection Agency (EPA) in March 1999 confirmed
what many environmentalists knew that forty per cent of group water
schemes in rural Ireland are contaminated with the E-coli bacteria which
makes the water unfit for human consumption.[4] E-coli is a coliform. It can

2. Don Hinrichsen, 'The Ocean Planet', *People and the Planet*, 1998, p 6-7.
3. Frank McDonald, 'Nitrate and phosphate over-use is blamed for coastal pollution', *Irish Times*, December 3 1997, p 10.
4. Liam Reid, 'E-coli in 40% of rural tap water', *The Sunday Tribune*, March 7, 1999, p 1.

cause serious illnesses like gastro-enteritis in humans. Old people and child-ren are particularly vulnerable.

The greenhouse effect

Chemical pollution is changing the structure of the earth's atmosphere, threatening to alter climate and expose human populations to higher levels of dangerous ultraviolet radiation. The atmospheric concentration of carbon dioxide, methane, chloroflourocarbons (CFCs) and other 'greenhouse' gases are expected to increase by thirty per cent during the next fifty years. This build-up is likely to increase the earth's surface temperature by between 1.5 and 4.5 degrees centigrade by the year 2030. This will cause major, and in the main, deleterious climatic changes. In northern latitudes, winters will probably be shorter and wetter, summers longer and drier. Sub-tropical areas might become drier and more arid and tropical ones wetter. The changes will have major, but as yet unpredictable, effects on agriculture and natural eco-systems.

As the oceans warm up and expand, sea levels will rise, leading to severe flooding over lowland areas. Much of Bangladesh and the low-lying areas in many countries will simply disappear. Storms of great ferocity, like hurricane Mitch that slammed into Central America in October 1998, will probably become more frequent. The people who will be most affected will be those who live in low lying areas like Bangladesh.

In the run up to the United Nations meeting on climate change in Kyoto, Japan, in December 1997, a group of almost 2000 scientists that comprise the Intergovernmental Panel on Climate Change (IPCC) called for a sixty per cent reduction in the use of fossil fuel. Unfortunately the politicians who attended the meeting could only agree to a miserly five to seven per cent reduction.

To date the churches in Ireland have not faced up to this global challenge even though more and more scientists are predicting that climate change will cause huge suffering for poor people. If Ireland continues with its present 'business as usual' approach to the burning of fossil fuel, we will fail to meet the obligations that we assumed at Kyoto. There ought to be a concerted effort to move away from fossil fuel and promote alternative sources of ener-gy like wind, water and wave power.

Effects of tropical deforestation

The destruction of the tropical forests has many adverse effects. Massive soil erosion results in a decrease in agricultural productivity and consequent mal-nutrition and even famine. The greatest tragedy of all is the mega-extinction of species which is following in the wake of the destruction of the forests. It is estimated that human activity is extinguishing species at '1,000 times the natural rate seen in evolution.[5] Already tens of thousands of species have been lost. E. O. Wilson, a Harvard biologist and author of *The Diversity of Life*, estimates that we are we are losing 27,000 species each year. Many would consider this to be a conservative estimate, but Wilson warns that the destruction of species will soar as the last remaining areas of tropical forests are exploited and destroyed.

If the present rate of extinction continues, fifty per cent or even more of all the life-forms on earth could be extinguished during the next few decades. Norman Myers, a British biologist and expert on tropical forests, considers that the present 'extinction spasm' is the greatest set back to life's abundance and diversity since the first flickering of life emerged almost four billion years ago. Extinction on such a scale is so horrendous that it is difficult to grasp. Many species are being pushed beyond the precipice of extinction before scientists have been able to identify them.

Because the reality of extinction and the process by which it is taking place is removed from us, our traditional human-centred moral categories fail to even register what is happening. Our present moral principles can deal in an adequate way with suicide, homicide and even genocide, but we have no way of dealing with biocide or geocide. The evil of species extinction does not appear, for example, in the encyclical *Veritatis Splendor* which was written by Pope John Paul II to restate Catholic moral teaching in the contemporary world.[6]

Extinction negates the labour, care, energy and untold experiments which were needed to bring forth this gorgeous earth with its great diversity of creatures. The irreversible destruction of life on a such a scale, within the past few decades, must be one of the most important ethical issues of our times. Yet it is seldom discussed in either secular or religious publications.

Given the history of forest exploitation, Irish people should be very sensitive to forest destruction. In 1600 over twelve per cent of the country was covered in broadleaf forests. The eighth century saw a concerted attack on Irish forest; by the time the Act of Union was passed in 1800 only two per cent of the country was covered in woodland. Since the foundation the state, the forest cover in Ireland has increased, but the bulk of the planting, unfortunately, is made up of conifers rather than broadleaf trees.

---

5. Tim Radford, 'Dead Zones in the oceans and a rate of extinction 1,000 times faster than evolution', *The Guardian*, August 3 1999.
6. *Veritatis Splendor*, The Catholic Truth Society, London, 1993.

It would also seem that we Irish have learned nothing from the forest mining that marred our own country during the second half of the present millennium. We are now the largest per capita importers of tropical wood in the EU. Imports grew a staggering sixty-four per cent during the decade between 1977 and 1987. Most of our tropical wood, especially iroko, (commonly called teak) comes from West Africa and, especially, the Ivory Coast where the forests are being logged in an unsustainable way. If the present rate of depletion continues, the forests there will be gone within five years. As far as I am aware there is no religious voice willing to challenge this plunder and shout stop. I have not heard a religious leader raising his/her voice in public support of the certification initiative of the international Forest Stewardship Council (FSC). This certification guarantees the consumer that wood which is purchases originated in a forest that is managed in a sustainable way and that those involved in logging and transporting are paid just wages. Despite the importance of trees in the biblical tradition, and the role of the cross in our redemption, contemporary Christians are oblivious to the present destruction of forests.

Waste and the disposable society

The unsustainability and vulnerability of our present day global industrial and commercial society is also very evident when one looks at it from the rubbish heaps which have continued to grow higher and higher in recent decades. A decade ago Newsweek (27 November 1989) portrayed the industrial world being 'buried alive' in garbage.

Increased levels of waste is becoming a major problem in Ireland. In 1998 each individual generated half a tonne of waste. Between 1984 and 1995 there was a sixty-two per cent increase in the level of household and commercial waste.[7] Ninety-two per cent of this waste ends up in landfills, but space is running out. Despite efforts by waste management groups to promote landfill options, very few communities want a 'super dump' in their backyard. As I write, the community in the picturesque village of Silvermines in North Tipperary are vigorously opposing the proposed mega-dump in their village.

Rates of recycling are very low in Ireland compared to other countries. Pope John Paul II has repeatedly made a connection between rampant consumerism and environmental destruction. In 1990 he wrote that:

Modern society will find no solution to the ecological problem unless it

---

7. Kevin O'Sullivan, 'Problems of the environment are intensifying – EPA' (Waste Production), *The Irish Times,* July 15 1999, p 14.

takes a serious look at its lifestyle. In many parts of the world society is given to instant gratification and consumerism while remaining indifferent to the damage which these cause ... simplicity, moderation and discipline, as well as a spirit of sacrifice, must become part of everyday life, lest all suffer the negative consequences of the careless habits of a few.[8]

In Ireland there has been very little effort by religious leaders to promote recycling, re-using goods or simple cutting down on our use of material things and linking this lifestyle change with traditional Christian asceticism.

The Irish environment

During the past twenty-five years, increased industrialisation and intensive agriculture have taken a huge toll on the Irish environment. The EPA report for 1998 concedes that Ireland's environmental problems are intensifying with economic growth. Their main worry is that environmental degradation might scupper the 'Celtic Tiger'.[9] Agricultural practices and thoughtless building programmes have silenced birds like larks, yellowhammers, corn buntings and corncrakes that brought joy to the hearts of previous generations of Irish people.

One could continue to give depressing examples of global and national environmental destruction. My aim in presenting the data above is to give a valid framework which will help us to truly appreciate the level of environmental damage globally and locally. I believe it now threatens the survival of many of the earth's creatures, in the short term, including human beings in the long-term. We must now interpret and critique this devastation of the earth in the light of the gospel and the resources of the Christian tradition.

Recent Catholic Church teaching

Despite the destruction which is taking place in our world, the churches have not responded in any effective way to environmental destruction. Let me illustrate what I am saying by a few quotations from recent Catholic Church teaching.

Vatican II is undoubtedly the major achievement of the Catholic Church in the twentieth century. *Gaudium et Spes* (The Pastoral Constitution on the Church in the Modern World) is a milestone in the history of the church's stance towards the world. It embodies a positive, liberating vision of life that refuses to seal off religious issues from the rest of human affairs. One cannot,

---

8. 'Peace with God the Creator, Peace with all Creation', Vatican City, January 1, 1990.
9. Kevin O'Sullivan, 'Problems of the environment are intensifying – EPA', *Irish Times*, July 15 1999, p 14.

however, argue that it is grounded in an ecological vision of reality. This document subscribes to what is called 'dominion theology': the natural world is there for man's exclusive use, 'for man, created in God's image, received a mandate to subject to himself all that it contains, and govern the world with justice and holiness.' (No. 34)

This anthropocentric bias is even more marked in No. 12 of the same document. It claims almost universal agreement for the teaching that 'according to the unanimous opinion of believers and unbelievers alike, all things on earth should be related to man as their centre and crown.' The cultures of tribal peoples and Hinduism and Buddhism, the great religions of the East, can hardly be used to bolster up this claim.

The first papal document devoted exclusively to environment and development issues, entitled *Peace with God the Creator, Peace with all creation,* was published on January 1, 1990. In it the Pope draws attention to the moral and religious dimensions of the environmental crisis. He declares that 'Christians, in particular realise that their duty towards nature and Creator are an *essential* part of their faith.' (No. 15, emphasis mine) This teaching is arguably the best kept secret in the Catholic Church globally and here in Ireland. I have seldom heard it being quoted.

It is also important to acknowledge that this document is heavily dependent on the *Justice, Peace and Integrity of Creation* (JPIC) programme, which the World Council of Churches launched at its Assembly in Vancouver in 1983. To its credit, the World Council of Churches is one of the few Christian institutions that has consistently focused its attention on ecology, development, justice and poverty during the past twenty-five years.

Given that the Christian churches have arrived at these challenges a little breathless and a little late, they must now make up for lost time and, in co-operation with other faiths, throw all their energies into urgently addressing the challenge of *Justice, Peace and the Integrity of Creation.* Unless this awareness is gained quickly, human beings and the rest of the planet's community will be condemned to live amid the ruins of the natural world.

How the churches might respond to environmental ruin
The first and most important contribution that the churches could make to the present ecological crisis would be to acknowledge the magnitude of the problem and urge people to face it with courage. Much of the data regarding the deteriorating state of our air, water, soils and tropical forests is now generally accepted by the scientific community. In November 1992 over 1,500 scientists, including many Nobel prize-winners, issued a wake-up call. They

stated that human beings and the natural world were on a collision course: 'No more than one or a few decades remain before the chance to avoid the threats we now confront will be lost.'

Need for a prophetic witness from the churches

Yet many Northern governments, and especially transnational corporations, who have benefited from the current shape of the global economy, are unwilling to acknowledge the extent of the problem and as a consequence change their ways. The inability of politicians at a national and global level to tackle the issue effectively is a case in point. As we saw earlier, the 2,000 scientists of Intergovernmental Panel on Climate Change (IPCC) called for a sixty per cent cut in emission of greenhouse gases in an effort to lessen the full impact of global warming. Corporate interests, especially in the coal, oil and automobile sectors, have lobbied very effectively to block any increase in taxes on fossil fuel or any serious effort to reduce greenhouse gas emissions in the US to 1990 levels by the year 2010. In the run-up to the Climate Change Convention in Kyoto in December 1997, the United States Congress resisted any initiative on a carbon tax. So while scientists are painting appalling scenarios, politicians, manipulated by the corporate world, are willing to adopt a wait-and-see attitude.

In the face of these efforts to downplay the seriousness of the climate change issue, the churches must be resolute in their determination to witness to the truth. Such a stand on behalf of the poor and the integrity of God's creation would be very much in line with the prophetic ministry of the scriptures. One is reminded of the responsibility of the watchman in the book of Ezekiel to alert the community in the time of danger:

> But if the watchman sees the sword coming and does not blow the trumpet, so that people are warned, and the sword comes, and takes any one of them; that man is taken away in his iniquity, but his blood I will require of the watchman's hand. (Ezek 33:6)

The World Council of Churches has responded to this crisis by publishing a very thorough analysis of the ecological, economic, ethical, theological and pastoral aspect of global warming in a document called *Sign of Peril, Test of Faith: Accelerated Climate Change*.[10] The text discussed the theological and ethical issues involved in global warming and attempted to motivate the churches to become involved in the issue. All the Christian churches should

---

10. *Signs of Peril, Test of Faith: Accelerated Climate Change*, World Council of Churches, 150, route de Ferney, PO Box 2100, 1221 Geneva 2, Switzerland, May 1994.

throw their moral authority behind this document. It is worth remembering that while church presence was very evident at the United Nations conference on population in Cairo (1995), there was hardly a word from religious leaders before, during or since Kyoto (December 1997), despite the fact that global warming will create misery for tens of millions of people.

Toward a theology and spirituality of creation
Another important contribution that the churches can make is to develop a spirituality of creation. In attempting to do this, Christian thinkers will find many helpful insights both in the biblical tradition and in different Christian spiritualities which have flourished, often, it must be admitted, at the margins, during the past two millennia. One thinks of the centrality of creation in both Celtic spirituality and the spirituality of St Francis of Assisi.

If this theology is to focus on the well-being of the total biosphere, or in theological terms, on all God's creation, then it will have to adopt what the Australian biblical theologian, Elaine Wainwright, has called a 'hermeneutics of reclamation', simply because much of the classical Christian tradition is very human centred.[11]

Genesis calls us to imitate a gracious God who loves Creation and cares for the earth
One could begin 'this hermeneutic of reclamation' right at the first line of Genesis. The Bible affirms that the world was created by a personal God who declares that it is good and who loves his creation (Gen 1:1). This is an extremely important statement, as many cultures in the ancient Near East believed that, since the earth was subject to decay, it must have been created, at least in part, by an evil spirit. This belief still lingers on even in the minds of people who profess to be Christian. It is one of the reasons why people who claim to be Christians can lay waste a forest or destroy fragile ecosystems without having the slightest twinge of conscience that what they are doing might be wrong.

The divine injunction to humankind in Gen 1:28, 'to increase and multiply and have dominion over the earth' is not a licence to exploit creation, though down through the centuries it has often been interpreted in that way. Nowadays scripture scholars argue that the commission, and especially the notion of dominion, originally was understood as a challenge to humans to imitate God's loving kindness and faithfulness and act as his viceroy in regard to the non-human component of the earth. Like the viceroys of the king, men and women are expected to be just, honest and render real service . The

11. Elaine Wainwright, 'A Metaphorical Walk through Scripture in an Ecological Age', *Pacifica*, Summer 1994, PO Box 271, Brunswick East, Victoria 3057, Australia.

virtues of the righteous king are portrayed in Ps 72:4-6. He will combine defence of the poor: 'may he defend the cause of the poor' (verse 4) with concern for the fertility of the land: 'may he be like rain that falls on the mown grass, like showers that water the earth' (verse 6).

In the Psalms (e.g. Ps 104) and Wisdom literature, especially the Book of Job, there is a clear appreciation that the *raison d'être* of creation is not found primarily in its ability to meet human needs. It has its own dignity, its own rights and reasons for being, quite apart from its role in sustaining humans. This is stated very clearly in the speeches of Yahweh in the Book of Job, chapters 38-41.

Furthermore, there is a strong sense of the interdependence of all creatures in Psalm 104. Ian Bradley, in *God is Green*, writes that in the Bible 'God is seen as the Lord of all creation' and that 'there is a strong sense of the interdependence of all creatures and an image of the world as a single cosmic community rather than (as) a collection of autonomous entities'.[12]

Stewardship

A theology of creation will also have to deal with the fact that human well-being, both for individuals and communities, depends on other creatures and a fertile environment. Here again the Bible has much to teach us in how to relate to the rest of creation. In chapters two and three of the Book of Genesis humans are challenged to be stewards of God's creation and to live in companionship with the rest of creation. The command of God to Adam and Eve is 'to till and to keep' (Gen 2:15).

For the People of Israel, the demands of stewardship are seen in the sensitive way they viewed the land. Aware of their origins as nomads and outcasts, they saw the land as a gift from God. Among the neighbours of Israel, the land was often seen as the exclusive property of the king or ruling classes (1 Kgs 21). This was not true in Israel. Land was the heritage of all the people and it was meant to sustain the whole community (Ex 19:5). But in a deeper way, Israel knew that she did not, in fact, own the land. Yahweh was the true land owner. The cultivators were only God's tenants; they were stewards and it was clearly recognised that there were certain restrictions on how they might utilise it:

> the land must not be sold in perpetuity, for the land belongs to me and to me you are only strangers and guests. (Lev 25:23)

The stewardship metaphor has sometimes been criticised as being exces-

---

12. Ian Bradley, *God is Green,* Darton, Longman and Todd, 1992, p 19.

sively human-centred and too simplistic for addressing complex ecological challenges.[13] Despite these reservations, the ideas and attitudes involved in stewardship have much to teach this generation. Modern mechanical agriculture that exploits land to the point of exhaustion in order to maximise short-term profits has much to re-learn from the wisdom contained in the Book of Leviticus.

I have come that they may have life and have it to the full. (Jn 10:10)
A Christian theology of creation has much to learn from the attitude of respect that Jesus displayed towards the natural world. He enjoyed an intimacy with nature which is evident from his parables – the sower and the seed (Mt 13:4-9, 18-23), the vine and the branches (Jn 15:1-17, Mk 12:1-12). He illustrated his stories by referring to the lilies of the field (Lk 12:27), the birds of the air (Mt 6:26) and foxes and their lairs (Lk 9:58).

In this age of unbridled consumerism, where greed is often represented as a virtue, it is important to remember that Jesus lived lightly on the earth. He warned his disciples against hoarding possessions and allowing their hearts to be enticed by the lure of wealth (Mt 6:19-21). It is clear that we will find no support in the teachings of Jesus for the modern throw-away, earth destroying consumer society.

For contemporary Christian living it is important to remember the centrality of Jesus is not confined to reflecting on his behaviour during his short life on earth in Palestine. We are resurrection people. Jesus is, as Paul tells us in Col 3:11, Eph 1:9-10 and many similar texts, the centre of human and cosmic history.

Jesus, as the Word and Wisdom of God, is active before the dawn of time bringing creation to birth out of the chaos. Through him the universe, the earth, and all life was created (Jn 1:3-5). All the rich unfolding of the universe – from the initial glow of the fireball – through the shaping of the stars and the earth as the green planet of the universe, right up to the emergence of humans and their varied cultures and histories, are centred on Jesus (Col 1:16-17).

Christians often make the mistake of thinking that the resurrection somehow catapults Jesus out of the order of creation and places him in some atemporal zone. The New Testament is adamant that the Risen Christ is even more deeply centred on all creation. The preface for the Mass of Easter Day

---

13. Clare Palmer 'Stewardship: a case study in environmental ethics' in Ian Hall, Margaret Goodall, Clare Palmer and John Reader (eds), *The Earth Beneant, A Critical Guide to Green Theology,* London, SPCK, 1992.

rejoices in the fact that the resurrection 'renews all creation'. In the context of extinction, it is important to remember that every living creature on earth has a profound relationship with the resurrected Lord. His loving touch heals our brokenness and fulfils all creation. So, to wantonly destroy any aspect of creation or to banish forever species from their place in the community of life is to deface the image of Christ which is radiated throughout our world.

An earth spirituality

The Bible vigorously denies that the world is evil. In chapter one of Genesis, God repeatedly contemplates what he has created and 'sees that it is good' (Gen 1:10, 18, 19, 21a and 26). It also affirms that the God whom we experience in our lives is not hiding in some inaccessible part of the universe. Creation is alive with the presence of God, if like the Psalmist, we look at it through the eyes of Faith:

The heavens are telling the glory of God;
And the firmament proclaims his handiwork.
Day to day pours forth speech,
And night to night declares knowledge. (Ps 19:1-2)

I believe an authentic creation spirituality would help regenerate Irish Christianity and, especially Irish Catholicism. Celtic spirituality celebrated the goodness of God that was manifested in the beauty of the world around us. Many Celtic monasteries were sited in remote and beautiful places like Skellig and Iona. It is no wonder that the monks came to love the cry of the curlew, the flight of the gannet, the bark of seals, the beauty of trees and wild flowers and the buzzing of bees and insects. Such a spirituality has much wisdom to offer to modern Ireland. It reminds us that we do not have a right to dominate and exploit nature without a thought for the consequence for other creatures and future generations.

Many Irish poets point in a similar direction. Patrick Kavanagh's poem 'The One' captures that special sense of God that comes to us in the few areas of relative wilderness that survive in modern Ireland:

Green, blue, yellow and red –
God is down in the swamps and marches
Sensational as April and almost incredible
the flowering of our catharsis ...

Renewing liturgy and devotions

The church should recognise the transformative power that liturgy and worship have in shaping individual and community values that promote justice and the integrity of creation. Good ritual can help communities evolve a new mode of human interaction with other human beings and with the natural world. Since the emergence of humankind on earth, people have always sought to link the deepest mysteries of their own personal and community life with the rhythms of the earth and cosmos through myths, rituals and ceremonies.

We need to be careful that our rituals are real. In November 1998 I attended a meeting called *Tionól 2000* where representatives from all the Irish dioceses gathered to prepare for the millennium. The theme of the liturgy on the Saturday night was drinking from our own wells. The idea behind the liturgy was that to move successfully into the new millennium we need to remember our past and be supported by it. Each delegation was encouraged to bring water from one of the holy wells in the diocese. At one level the ritual was very moving: it was rich in Gaelic themes and songs and the movement patterns drew the congregation from the past into the future. However, the liturgy never adverted to the fact that water from most of these wells is no longer potable. This oversight turned what could have been a very powerful liturgy to heal and reclaim the waters of Ireland into something superficial. I found it somewhat disquieting that a national church meeting centred on initiatives for the millennium was not much more sensitive to environmental challenges and especially the poisoning of Irish waters.

Sacraments

The sacramental liturgy of the church offers many moments in which the Christian community can experience the presence of God in the world of nature. In the Catholic liturgy we are incorporated into the church through the sacrament of baptism. The symbolism of baptism revolves around life-giving water and the power of the Spirit to transform the lives of individuals and whole communities. These ought to act as a strong incentive for the Christian community to ensure that their water and the waters in their locality are not polluted with toxic, human, industrial and agricultural waste. Baptism initiates people into the Christian community. In the light of our contemporary understanding of the place of humans within the wider earth-community, and of the extensive destruction of this community at the hands of humans, it would be helpful to understand the sacrament of baptism, not merely as an initiation into the Catholic Church, but as an initiation into the wider earth and cosmic community.

Eucharist

The eucharist is also pregnant with all kinds of creative possibilities for deepening our awareness of the holy communion which unites God, humankind, other creatures and all creation. In the eucharist the elements of bread and wine, taken from the earth and transformed by human labour, are offered in the memory of the passion, death and resurrection of Jesus, and through the action of the Spirit they are transformed into the Body and Blood of Christ. The experience of eucharist is a spur to Christians to work for a just, compassionate, sharing society. It also summons Christians to work for a sustainable society where seeds and soils are protected and the bonds of interdependence between humans and the rest of creation are more clearly understood and experienced. The eucharist is that holy communion in which all the members give themselves to one another in order to promote abundant life for all.

Promoting and preparing for a new, sustainable culture
Moving beyond liturgy, environmental issues must become part of the wider ministry of the church. It is sad and ironic that the present ecological crisis is the result of considerable human success. Everyone will admit that greed, covetousness and other commonly recognised human vices have undoubtedly contributed to our present crisis. Nevertheless, the principle cause of ecological devastation in our world today has been the unrelenting pursuit of what many people consider a good and desirable thing – the modern, growth-oriented, industrial model of development. What many people feel is the good life, something to be aspired to and worked for, is in fact destroying the world.

The economic boom in Ireland since the mid-1990s, with GDP growth rates of between six and nine per cent, has taken a huge toll on the environment. Even someone like the former Taoiseach, Dr Garret FitzGerald, whose interests lie more in the economic field than the ecological one, believes that 'the Celtic tiger threatens to devour Ireland's much-hyped pristine environment'. (*The Irish Times*, May 26 1997)

The churches must work assiduously with all those who are attempting to oppose this destructive way of living and espouse a more compassionate and sustainable culture that will support and enhance all life. The Dominican Sisters are to be commended for not selling seventy acres of prime land in the vicinity of Wicklow. Instead they have transformed it into a biodynamic enterprise with a wild-life sanctuary and an ecology centre.[14] It would be a wonderful millennial initiative if other Religious Orders who still own land followed this creative example.

To date only one Irish Bishop, Bishop Bill Murphy of Kerry, has tackled the environmental issue in a pastoral letter.[15] Given the environmental chal-

---

14. Eilis Ryan 'Saving the Earth', *The Farmers Journal*, May 15 1999, p 3.
15. Bishop Bill Murphy, *Going to the Father's House. A Jubilee People*, Pastoral Letter to the Diocese of Kerry 1999.

lenge globally and nationally, the fact that the leadership of the Irish church has not addressed its moral and religious implications is, in my mind, a major failure in terms of effective episcopal leadership.

The Irish bishops could perform a great service both for the Irish people and the environment by initiating a national dialogue about the environment. This process ought to be carried out on an ecumenical basis. The Pope's 1990 letter recognises the potential for 'a vast field of ecumenical and inter-religious co-operation' around environmental questions. Such discussion at local and national level might well flower into a powerful pastoral letter.

But we will need more than talk. As chair of the environmental organisation VOICE, I know that the voluntary environmental community is weak and so poorly resourced that it may not survive long into the new millennium. Yet much of the public policy changes in the area of water, waste and genetic engineering has been as a result of effective lobbying by An Taisce, EarthWatch, Genetic Concern and VOICE. If these organisations go under because of lack of support this crucial voice will be silenced. Diocesan and religious congregations must increase their support for environmental organisations. One major need at the moment is accessible and cheap office space in Dublin. Many convents and seminaries are now empty. One way of using them for the common good would be to rent space at low rates to environmental groups.

The call to renew the earth

One important Christian notion captures the urgency of the task that faces us. There are a number of words in Greek for time – *chronos* and *kairos*. *Chronos* captures the notion of counting time in some orderly way. The New Testament seldom uses this word; it prefers to use the word *kairos*. *Kairos* denotes a special moment which, in fact, is a time of crisis. The antipathy between the forces of good and evil have reached a climax and people are challenged to make a choice. The ultimate resolution of the conflict is assured since Yahweh is in charge of the world, but the challenges presented demand the active involvement of believers. For many individuals and groups this will mean a conversion experience.

The ecological crisis is such a *kairos* moment. Unless positive choices are made now, irreversible damage will be done to the earth's fabric. Responding to the challenge will demand concrete choices for individuals and institutions to help bring about this new age. The church, which Vatican II sees 'as a sign raised up among the nations', should be in the forefront in trying to usher in this new ecological age where a mutually enhancing relationship ought to exist between humankind and the rest of creation.

Ireland in the New Millennium:
A Brooder or a Gloater?*

Mary Sutton

Introduction

Some thirty five years ago, Conor Cruise O'Brien, discussing the workings of the United Nations, distinguished between nations that were instinctively imperial and those that instinctively identified with the oppressed. He styled them respectively the 'gloaters' and the 'brooders'.[1]

At that time there would have been no doubt about where Ireland stood. The historical legacy of colonisation, famine and relative poverty by Western standards, placed Ireland squarely in the 'brooders' division.

Today, while the historical legacy and problems of poverty remain, the astonishingly rapid pace of economic growth, and the tumultuous social change of the last thirty years, beg the question: does the Celtic Tiger aspire to leave the ranks of the downtrodden but worthy 'brooders' to join the smug, self-satisfied 'gloaters'?

What is Ireland's stance today in relation to the developing world and what does this suggest for the role Ireland will play in international relations in the new Millennium?

The roots of empathy

Much of the inspiration for Ireland's early interventions in the field of international development co-operation drew explicitly on Ireland's own historical experience. Seven hundred years of colonisation made Ireland unique among the members of the OECD, the rich countries' club. Ireland perceived itself and was perceived by many developing countries as having a special understanding of the colonised countries of Africa, Asia and Latin America that rendered it uniquely placed among rich countries. While others could be assumed to have self-interested motives in relation to developing countries, Ireland's motives were pure. The Irish struggle for independence and the successful establishment of a republic was seen as an example and inspiration to many of the newly independent countries of the south including India.

---

* I would like to thank Maura Leen for her very helpful comments on an earlier draft.
1. Conor Cruise O'Brien, *To Katanga and Back,* Four Square Books, 1965, p 45.

The experience of the Famine also made Ireland unique in Europe and created a folk memory that was seen as a powerful incentive for Irish people to be particularly responsive to the needs of Southern countries facing famine in modern times. The fact that Ireland was still a largely agricultural country and a small, open economy in the 1960s also suggested points of similarity and scope for the transfer of skills.

At the time of the 150th anniversary of the Great Hunger there was debate as to whether it really was the folk memory of famine or the long tradition of missionary involvement, particularly in Africa, that best explained the enormous generosity of Irish people in responding to, for example, the Ethiopian famine of the mid-1980s. The missionary links stretch back into the latter decades of the nineteenth century. By the mid 1960s there were over 60 Irish mission societies with almost 8,000 personnel working in Africa, Asia and Latin America. In the 1960s and 1970s NGOs such as Gorta, Concern, Trócaire and Goal became active in supporting projects and programmes in developing countries and responding to emergency situations.

So, at least at a superficial level, there seemed to be a case for a high degree of empathy and solidarity between Ireland and the countries of the South. When it came to concrete expressions of commitment to redress international imbalances and inequities, how did Ireland's performance match up to the rhetoric?

From empathy to practical help
Ireland still has strong links with the developing world through its missionaries and its Non-Governmental Organisations. While the number of missionaries has fallen since the 1960s, in 1996 there were still almost 4,000 Irish missionaries in 93 countries.[2] In addition to pastoral work, missionary personnel are engaged in education, healthcare, community development and social work. Aid delivered via Irish NGOs has been measured at 0.1% of GNP. This is by far the highest contribution of any of the rich countries and is five times the average. This level of involvement by missionaries and NGOs, is remarkable by any standards and bears witness to a long-standing and profound commitment by Irish people to issues of poverty reduction and development in the south.

At the official level, Ireland had begun to make contributions to United Nations agencies and funds in the early 1950s. The international target for Official Development Assistance adopted in 1970, set out the expectation

---

2. Irish Missionary Union, *Survey of Overseas Personnel*, 1996, p 2.

that each 'First World' country would contribute 0.7% of its GNP per annum in aid. Up to 1973 the Irish attitude to the target was that we would play our part 'as our resources permitted' but that the 0.7% target was far too demanding for a country at Ireland's stage of development. It was contended that a target of 0.2% or 0.3% would be appropriate for 'countries like us'.[3]

It was not until the mid 1970s that there developed a policy and a discretionary commitment of resources to the area of Official Development Assistance. Ireland's joining the EEC in 1973 involved greater mandatory contributions to development co-operation programmes. It also meant that Ireland had joined a 'rich man's club' whose members had extensive historical ties with developing countries and well established and resourced bilateral aid programmes. There would be expectations of Ireland in this area but there would also be extensive opportunities to influence decisions that would have a major impact on developing countries. At the foundation of Trócaire in February 1973, the Bishops of Ireland noted in their Pastoral Letter that 'As members of the world's most powerful trading group, we will have an opportunity of helping the needy nations in a manner and on a scale never within our power before. It is our duty to ensure that our public representatives influence that great body in the right direction.'[4]

In 1973/4, alongside the mandatory payments to United Nations bodies and the newly acquired responsibilities to contribute to EEC development co-operation budgets, a Bilateral Aid Programme was established focused on four priority countries in Africa; the Agency for Personal Service Overseas was established and a target for Ireland's ODA was set such that resources were to be allocated in 'a planned manner over a number of years'. The aspiration was to reach 0.35% of GNP or half the UN target by the end of the decade. In the event ODA as a % of GNP climbed slowly to 0.25% of GNP by the mid-80s before falling back to 0.16% in 1992. Since then it has been on an upward trend with substantial annual increases in monetary terms. However, because the rate of growth of GNP has been so rapid in recent years, these increases have not translated into the promised rapid progress towards the UN target. The ratio for 1999 is likely to be 0.33%.[5]

In terms of quality, Ireland's aid has always been authentically focused on the alleviation of poverty. Almost 90% of the total goes to the poorest countries which is the second highest proportion among the OECD donors; it is on grant rather than loan terms and it is untied except for technical co-operation

3. *Parliamentary Debates, Dáil Éireann, Official Report,* Vol 257, p 214, 1971.
4. Bishops of Ireland on Development, February 2, 1973, para. 15.
5. Parliamentary Question No.81 (Ref No. 12034/99) 11 May, 1999.

which is tied to personnel. It is largely expended on basic needs such as education, healthcare, water and agriculture.

It was a very long time before the philosophy and ethos of the Irish aid programme was spelled out. However, the Irish Aid Strategy Plan 1993-7 and the White Paper on Foreign Policy published in 1996 went a long way towards remedying this omission. While recognising that development co-operation is often treated as synonymous with aid, these policy documents emphasise the breadth of development interests and the interlinkages between trade, aid, debt, finance and other facets of foreign policy. The White Paper argued that the ideals of development co-operation should permeate all other aspects of foreign policy and that there should be coherence between the various policy elements such that they reinforced rather than undermined each other.

The emphasis in the aid expenditure on basic needs has been complemented in recent years by a robust commitment to the area of human rights. The portfolio of the Minister of State responsible for Development Co-operation now also includes in its title human rights. There now exists a special Human Rights Unit and an Interdepartmental Committee on Human Rights as well as a Department of Foreign Affairs/NGO Joint Standing Committee on Human Rights. Thus, the Irish aid programme could be said to exemplify a broad commitment to the whole gamut of human rights. Political and civil rights are underpinned by providing support and training to countries embarking on multiparty elections and by training in areas of law and civic administration. Social and economic rights are supported by the practical assistance to health, education and food security projects provided via the official aid programme. In this sense, the Irish aid programme demonstrates a commitment to poverty alleviation, basic needs and human rights, a spectrum increasingly referred to as 'development rights'.

The Irish government has become increasingly active in relation to the issue of the debt burden of the developing countries. The publication in September 1998 of a joint policy statement on Third World debt from the Departments of Foreign Affairs and Finance was something of an innovation. While the NGO community opposed the allocation of resources to the Enhanced Structural Adjustment Facility of the International Monetary Fund, it welcomed the statement of principles underlying debt policy. The government was seen to take a proactive stance on a key issue for many developing countries. Cynics might say that the debt issue is a no, or low, cost issue for Ireland given that we are not a creditor country and therefore do not stand to lose from any concessions agreed. Furthermore, it is an issue where leadership from the NGO sector has mobilised Irish public opinion to the extent that some 750,000 Irish people signed the Jubilee 2000 petition calling for the G8 countries to act to 'break the chains of debt'. Nonetheless, as with human rights, Ireland has worked to develop a credible approach to a complex and crucial issue.

The limits of empathy

After almost three decades of effort, Ireland has not yet reached half the UN target for ODA and is still below the OECD average. However, because ODA from many other OECD countries has been in decline for some years, Ireland's relative position on the donor league table has improved. Having languished at the bottom for many years, Ireland now ranks joint tenth of the twenty-one countries that are members of the Development Assistance Committee of the OECD.[6] The trailblazers continue to be the three Scandinavian countries and the Netherlands, all four of whom have exceeded the UN target. The laggards are the United States (whose ODA has fallen to 0.12% of GNP) and Italy. Ireland's aspiration continues to be to reach an interim target of 0.45% of GNP and anticipates reaching at least 0.36% by 2001.[7]

Paradoxically, while the excuse for not reaching the UN target in the 1970s and 1980s was Ireland's relative poverty – it was not a suitable target for 'countries like us' – today the excuse is Ireland's relative prosperity. It is argued that it is unreasonable to expect a country whose GNP is growing as rapidly as Ireland's to allocate the level of resources needed to make a greater impact on the ODA target. However, the target was set in terms of a percentage of GNP precisely to require an equivalent level of commitment and cost of each donor country. A proportion of national resources was to be set aside to contribute to narrowing the gap between living standards in the rich one-third and poor two-thirds of the world.

It is well recognised that ideals are only robust if they can withstand the challenge of self interest. Lofty aspirations in relation to poverty alleviation in the developing world are routinely rendered hollow when protectionist instincts keep out of Northern markets the very goods whose production aid programmes have supported. The classic case is textiles but in Ireland and elsewhere agricultural produce are regularly at the forefront of efforts to maintain jobs and incomes at home even at the expense of the livelihoods of those much worse off. Despite the global trend towards liberalisation of

6. All cross country comparisons are for 1997 as published by the OECD in *Development Cooperation – Efforts and Policies of the Members of the Development Assistance Committee*, 1998
7. Parliamentary Question, op. cit.

economies, the EU continues to be highly protectionist in relation to imports such as bananas and beef.[8]

In Ireland's case in the recent past the issue of refugees and asylum seekers has been an uncomfortable reminder of the 'not in my back yard' syndrome. When the White Paper on foreign policy was published just a few short years ago, this issue was couched almost entirely in the context of dealing with the plight of refugees and internally displaced people within the developing world. The growth in the number of refugees and asylum seekers arriving in Ireland in the last two to three years has focused attention on this issue. The debate has been harsh and discordant in many respects. The government has rowed back on the commitments in the 1996 Refugee Act which it now considers to have been too liberal, and that Act is currently under review.

The unanticipated increase in the numbers seeking asylum in Ireland put great strain on the administrative procedures and practices in operation in the Department of Justice. But equally it put a strain on attitudes and self-image. There has always in Ireland been a very high level of public support for development assistance and an exceptionally generous response to appeals from aid agencies, as well as a pride in the absence of racism and the hospitality offered to the stranger. When the number of refugees and asylum seekers grew from a few hundred to the current 6,000 or so, some of the media coverage was highly inflammatory. Headlines included 'Refugees Spark Housing Crisis', 'Crackdown on 2000 Sponger Refugees' and perhaps the most offensive of all, 'Refugee Rapists on the Rampage'. The incidence of verbal abuse and racist attacks suffered by individual refugees also gave the lie to the smug self-image. A survey of 157 asylum-seekers in 1999 found that virtually all the African respondents has been verbally abused and more than one-fifth had been physically assaulted.[9]

In their joint policy document on refugees and asylum seekers, the Irish Commission for Justice and Peace and Trócaire pointed out that: 'Ireland's support for many human rights issues in other countries now faces a credibility test at home. Our approach to refugees is a key yardstick on which to judge the consistency of our human rights standards. The refugee situation represents the clearest possible interface between foreign and domestic human rights policy. If we deny refugee status to genuine asylum seekers it will be difficult for Ireland to be credible in calling for an end to the conditions and situations which created such refugees in the first place.'[10]

8. *The Economist,* May 22, 1999, p 104.
9. A survey by the Pilgrim House community quoted in the *Irish Times,* April 24, 1999, p 9.
10. Irish Commission for Justice and Peace and Trócaire, *Refugees and Asylum Seekers – A Challenge to Solidarity,* 1997, p 11.

Reforming the national self-image

Looking forward to the new century, certain adjustments to Ireland's self-image in the field of international relations are necessary. First, Ireland is indisputably a rich country, capable of being a leader rather than a laggard in relation to the UN target for ODA. The old excuses of relative poverty within the OECD were hollow in the 1970s and 1980s when Ireland regularly ranked in the mid twenties in the world league table of almost 200 countries. By 1997 Ireland was the nineteenth richest country in the world in terms of GNP per capita and seventeenth in terms of the Human Development Index. This latter measure, developed by the United Nations Development Programme, is a composite measure taking account of factors such as life expectancy and educational attainment as well as income. The current day argument that it is our rapid rate of economic growth that prevents us from meeting our international obligations in this area is wholly disingenuous.

In relation to the debate on refugees and asylum seekers, there is clearly a need to put in place policies and procedures that meet Ireland's international obligations in this area and that provide a fair and transparent process for each individual applicant. It is interesting to note that in the national discourse refugees and asylum seekers are distinguished from mere 'economic migrants'. No such distinction seemed necessary when discussing the Irish diaspora.

It has long been recognised that public education in support of global citizenship and interdependence is a necessary element in creating and maintaining a constituency for aid. Indeed, during her Presidency of Ireland, Mary Robinson described human rights education as 'The Fourth "R"' – the fourth pillar of education along with reading, writing and arithmetic.'[11] It is now an urgent priority in Ireland to provide education in relation to multiculturalism and multi-ethnicity. The prevailing attitude to date has been to view refugees and asylum seekers as a problem and a burden rather than recognising the contribution that they can make to Irish society. It may be the case, indeed, that the needs of the Celtic Tiger for low cost labour will ultimately be met by allowing refugees and asylum seekers to work and by adopting more liberal attitudes to economic migrants.

Another area where the rather smug certainties of a few years ago have been punctured is in relation to the arms trade. It was Ireland's proud boast that it had done a greatly disproportionate amount to advance the cause of

---

11. 'Human Rights Education – the Fourth "R"', Address by the President of Ireland, Mary Robinson, to the Third International Meeting of the International Confederation of Principals in Boston on 23 July 1997.

disarmament at the UN over many years and that Ireland itself had no indigenous arms industry. The latter claim has been challenged in recent years as evidence has emerged of production in Ireland under licence of so-called dual use goods.

Similarly, the badge of neutrality was proudly worn and advanced as another reason why Ireland had a particularly good rapport with many of the countries of the South. In the post Cold War world and since the Treaties of Maastricht and Amsterdam, this argument, never very strong, has become redundant. The debate within Europe on a Common Foreign and Security Policy and the government's decision to join the Partnership for Peace have necessitated a reconceptualisation of Ireland's role. A key challenge, particularly following the Balkans War, will be to discern how Ireland can best contribute to peace and security within Europe and beyond. Ireland's current bid to become a member of the United Nations Security Council is a welcome indication of a wish to take a leadership role in international affairs.

Conclusion

So what is the national mindset as we enter the new millennium? Do we still see ourselves positively as generous, welcoming, fair, favouring the underdog and contributing on the world stage disproportionately to our size? How do we deal with the dissonance evident in recent years around the issue of refugees and asylum seekers? How do we justify our improved, but still poor, performance in relation to ODA? Are we mindful of our own history and empathetic because of it? Or are we rapidly leaving our past behind and becoming increasingly secular, materialistic and self-centred? In the globalised economy, is our only concern to ensure that we are in the winners enclosure?

Surely, this dichotomy is too stark. It will not be a case of flipping at a moment in time from the 'brooders' camp to the 'gloaters' camp. Rather we will adapt and develop a set of values to suit the new circumstances and the new time.

While on the one hand, the issues of international relations are becoming increasingly complex and demanding, Ireland's integration within the EU means that many of the key development related issues such as trade policy are decided at European level. What role will Ireland play in an EU that may grow to have twenty five or more members in the coming decades? The enormous internal transfers, from which Ireland benefited so greatly over the last quarter century, will be increasingly redirected towards newer members perhaps in Central and Eastern Europe. Hopefully, Ireland will be a strong voice encouraging the EU to adopt an outward looking stance and to play a constructive role in development co-operation.

The same values that we choose to adopt in relation to our policy choices nationally will inform our choices in relation to development co-operation. The evidence suggests that those countries that perform best in relation to poverty reduction at home are among the best performers in relation to ODA. For example, the United Nations Development Programme's measure of poverty and deprivation in industrialised countries scores Sweden and the Netherlands best and the United States worst – a ranking that mirrors their ODA performance.[12]

Will we in Ireland develop a social infrastructure with the same urgency as we develop our economic infrastructure? Will we be concerned to create an inclusive, participative, equitable society at home? If so, then it is likely that we will be committed to closing the gap in living standards and life chances internationally. We will view Official Development Assistance as a logical extension of social welfare at home and make rapid progress towards the UN target. Out of our commitment to human rights internationally we will contribute to the development of a global ethic.

We have the opportunity to grow beyond either the 'brooder' or the 'gloater' to integrate the best of our particular legacy with the more recent economic success to build a mature, cohesive society and to act as a capable, enthusiastic and responsible global citizen.

---

12. United Nations Development Programme, *Human Development Report 1998*, p 28, table 1.8.

Marriage in Ireland Today

Garret FitzGerald

INTRODUCTION

The ethical systems evolved by different elements of the human race have ultimately been based upon some concept of what is good for the health, happiness and above all survival of their communities. In some instances, distorted superstitions have led particular communities or civilisations to develop perverse views of how these objectives can best be achieved: for example, the Aztecs convinced themselves that huge numbers of human sacrifices were necessary for the good of their community. But the more advanced religions, basing their ethics upon rational perceptions of the ultimate interests of their communities, or even in some cases of the human race in general, developed well-balanced ethical systems of great sophistication – none more so than Christianity, I believe.

Of course, so far as marriage is concerned, the Christian Church did not invent the concept of monogamy, which was already the norm both in the Jewish and Greek cultures and in the Roman State within which Christianity developed. But the Christian Church emphatically endorsed this concept, emphasised the idea of indissolubility, and sacralised the marriage contract. As many other cultures have done, Christianity saw indissoluble monogamy as providing the optimal conditions for the upbringing of future generations of the human race, the members of which, to a degree unique amongst other living species, require both physically and psychologically a very prolonged period of nurture by their progenitors.

It is arguable, of course, that some of the specific provisions that the Christian Church later came to apply to marriage were too specifically linked to contemporary social conditions at various stages of its history – particularly during the prolonged post-Constantinian millennium when civil society had conceded to the church a monopoly of the solemnisation of marriage. Moreover, as in the course of its history the Christian Church faced particular situations, such as the prevalence of clandestine unions of uncertain validity in the sixteenth century, or of unions with non-Christians at the geographical margins of Christendom, it was tempted to adopt some specific positions that were difficult to reconcile with its own well-developed philosophy of marriage.

As I shall later suggest, by virtue of their anomalous character, some of these provisions or expedients have tended to weaken the church's authority in marital matters, while others have failed to mesh in satisfactorily with the emergence of parallel structures of civil marriage. Because of the rigidities and innate conservatism of its elaborate system of canon law, the Roman Catholic Church, in particular, has in my view been unwisely slow about adjusting to these new circumstances in the interest of sustaining the permanence of the marriage bond.

Nevertheless, despite these difficulties and problems, and despite the manner in which, during the last two centuries, state authorities have found it expedient to introduce provisions for the dissolution of civil marriages in various circumstances, the concept of marriage that emerged in Christendom over many centuries has in fact been largely retained within post-Christian Western societies.

Latterly, however, the role of marriage has come to be increasingly challenged, and in some cases even abandoned, at least provisionally, by significant proportions of the populations of Western societies. And, during the closing decades of the century now ending, this development has spread to Ireland.

But because in Ireland this development had been relatively recent, and because moreover many aspects of sexual behaviour tend of their nature to be private, and consequently poorly documented, the significance of the changes affecting marriage that have recently been taking place in this country have hitherto been poorly recognised and inadequately debated. This paper represents an attempt to fill some of these gaps, in the hope of promoting some rational and constructive discussion and debate on current issues relating to marriage in Ireland. Having outlined some of the relevant demographic data relating to marriage and births, both marital and non-marital, some issues are raised about possible action in the future that might tend to moderate some of what appear to be negative developments of recent decades.

STABILITY OF MARRIAGES AND BIRTHS UNTIL 1960

During most of the first two-thirds of the present century marriage and birth rates in Ireland remained relatively stable – albeit at levels that diverged markedly from the European norm. The Irish marriage rate was abnormally low (averaging just under 5.5 per thousand population), primarily because the proportion of those surviving in Ireland who never married was abnormally high, at about 25%. Moreover those who did marry, tended to marry late.

Nevertheless, despite this abnormal marriage pattern, an exceptional rate of marital fertility provided Ireland with a high marital birth rate – substantially above that of most of the rest of Europe. By contrast, the Irish non-marital birth rate was extraordinarily low, the proportion of births falling into this category having dropped during the middle decades of the century from 3.5% to a phenomenally low 1.5%. Moreover, because artificial contraceptives were not available, (around the time when they might have come into use on a significant scale in Ireland, viz. the mid-1930s, they were banned by law), and because abortion was not available in Ireland, this extraordinarily low non-marital birth rate can be taken as reflecting a genuinely very low level of non-marital sexual intercourse.

The potential impact of a very high marital fertility rate upon the Irish population level was more than offset not just by the low marriage rate but even more so by an exceptionally high rate of emigration combined with a poor survival rate amongst the younger generation. This latter phenomenon reflected a combination of high (albeit gradually declining) post-natal and neo-natal death rates as well as a high death rate amongst young people, the latter being occasioned by the prevalence of TB during the first half of the century.

The high early death rate, which continued, albeit to a diminishing extent, until after the middle of this century, has been persistently underestimated as a factor contributing to the decline in the Irish population. For, amongst those born even as late as the 1930s, the proportion of those remaining in Ireland who failed to survive beyond age 35 was almost one in six. When combined with the emigration of over one-third of that generation, this high death rate amongst the young population ensured that, despite exceptionally high marital fertility, the post-Famine decline in the Irish population persisted in the Irish State until the start of the 1960s.

To a considerable extent this abnormal demography was a consequence of slow economic growth – a phenomenon which persisted throughout the first four decades of Irish independence. A combination of factors, some of them beyond the control of any Irish government, contributed to this slow economic growth, and to its demographic consequences.

First, there was the fact that the only market open to Irish producers of either industrial or agricultural goods was that of Great Britain, the economy of which had, since the late nineteenth century, been growing much more slowly than the economies of the rest of the industrialised world. Moreover, continued economic dependence on the British market was peculiarly damaging in the Irish case because of the additional negative impact of Britain's 'cheap food' policy upon a still largely agricultural neighbour. For it must be remembered that as late as the end of the Second World War half of those at work in the Irish State were engaged in what in these external market conditions could only be an unremunerative and depressed farm sector.

This inherently depressed economic situation had been, moreover, artifi-

cially aggravated by an essentially futile attempt to exclude foreign investment in industry and to achieve self-sufficiency within a very small economy
that had a limited climatic range. These policies were especially counter-
productive when pursued in a small country where a reasonable standard of
living could be achieved only by earning through exports the means of
importing the huge range of goods which it was either climatically impossible
for it to produce, or which, by virtue of the minuscule size of its domestic
market, could be manufactured at home only at prohibitively high cost.

This is not the place to pursue in any detail the remarkable impact on
Irish economic growth of the reversal in the late 1950s of these counter-productive policies under favourable external conditions of freer trade and at a
time of rapidly expanding foreign investment. It is sufficient to remark that
nowhere else in the industrialised world in the second half of this century has
there been a change of economic circumstances anything like as dramatic as
in the Irish case.

The almost overnight post-1960 shift of the Irish economy from virtual
economic stagnation – unique in the Europe of its time – to a growth rate
which by the mid-1970s had come to exceed that of the remainder of the
EU, was bound to have huge consequences for Irish society. It is in fact in no
way surprising that during the final one-third of the twentieth century the
Irish State has experienced an unparalleled pace of change in its demography
and in its society – one for which, because of the earlier economic stagnation
and related stability in social mores, it was exceptionally ill-prepared. (Other
factors that had sheltered Ireland from changes occurring elsewhere had been
its neutrality during World War II and the conservative influence of the
Roman Catholic Church, including that institution's influence on public
policies such as film and book censorship and the banning of contraception
and divorce.)

It is against this unique background that marriage in Ireland today must
be viewed.

DEMOGRAPHIC CONSEQUENCES OF POST-1960 ECONOMIC GROWTH 1961-1981

a. Fall in: emigration
The first consequence of the shift from virtual economic stagnation in the
1950s to a 4.25% average growth rate was a sharp drop in emigration. Indeed
in the 1970s this led to a temporary reversal of the net outflow, for, although
the flow of migration for employment remained predominantly outbound,
the wives and families brought here by several tens of thousands of emigrants
returning to employment here shifted the overall balance of movement in the
reverse direction.

The impact of this fall in emigration, (together with the mid-century fall in the death rate of young people) was such that whereas in 1970 only 49% of those born in Ireland in 1935 were still alive and in Ireland, no less than 85% of those born a quarter-of-a century later, viz. in 1960, were alive in 1995. In other words, the proportion surviving in Ireland to age 35 rose during this twenty-five year period by almost three-quarters – because for this age cohort the toll of net emigration plus early deaths had been reduced by well over two-thirds.

Those two birth years – 1935 and 1960 – represent the extremes of this comparison. Those born in the years immediately following 1960 were harder hit by the recession of the early 1980s and by the temporary recurrence of large-scale emigration in the latter part of that decade, although this cohort has also benefited more from the employment boom of the 1990s, which has brought many of them back to Ireland in the last few years.

b. Increase in number of young people
Between 1961 and 1981 the post-1960 economic recovery had the effect of increasing by an astonishing 72% the number of young people in their twenties living in the state. During this initial period of economic growth, whilst economic conditions were accelerating the move from a late-marrying rural society to an earlier-marrying urban one, attitudes towards the institution of marriage remained largely unchanged. Moreover, within that urban society, employment at reasonable pay rates was at this period fairly readily available (*vide* the temporary emergence of net immigration in the 1970s) and house prices remained low in real terms because of the ready availability of privately-owned housing due to the earlier population decline.

c. Jump in the marriage rate
In these favourable conditions, the annual number of marriages increased by one-half between 1961 and 1974, and by 1981 the number of women aged 20-24 who were married had jumped by an astonishing 160%, while the number married aged 25-29 had also more than doubled.

d. Rise in the birth rate
This huge increase in the number of young married couples had evident potential implications for the marital birth rate, although a powerful counter-balancing factor was the emergence of contraception as a significant demographic factor from the mid-1960s onwards. Initially this development took the form of the contraceptive pill, but during the 1970s artificial contraceptives came increasingly into use and, as a result, by 1981 marital fertility had declined by about one-third. Consequently, instead of the total number of marital births rising from under 60,000 to over 100,000 during this period,

as would have happened had marital fertility remained at the level of the mid-1960s, the increase in such births following this very large increase in the number of young married couples, was less than 10,000.

However, by 1981 the number of young married couples had levelled off, and thereafter a combination of an acceleration of the decline in marital fertility and the emergence of a sharp drop in the marriage rate led, within fourteen years, to a virtual halving of the number of marital births.

e. Rise in non-marital births

Before addressing in more detail these post-1981 developments, reference must, however, be made to the increase in non-marital births which also followed the mid-1960s emergence of contraception as a significant factor in Irish demography. As mentioned earlier, the proportion of births that were non-marital had fallen from around 3.5% in the 1930s and 1940s to 1.5% in 1961 – viz. to under 1,000 a year – and even as late as 1966 the proportion was still not much over 2%. However, during the following fifteen years this ratio had increased to over 5%. Given that the number of young single women had also increased in this period by almost one-quarter, this represented rather more than a doubling of the ratio of such births to the numbers in the relevant female age-group (15-39). Nevertheless, the proportion of single women in this age-group giving birth to a child in 1981 was still only 1.25% of the women in this age cohort.

Some of the radical demographic changes that have marked the last two decades certainly found their origins back in the late 1970s. Nevertheless, despite the dramatic impact of contraception on marital fertility during the late 1960s and the 1970s, and the emergence in the 1970s of a flow of women to Britain in search of abortions, which was rising at an even faster rate than the increase in non-marital births, the working of society, in terms of the maintenance of traditional family structures, did not appear to most contemporaries to have been seriously weakened during that initial period of economic growth. It is largely during the 1980s that potentially de-stabilising developments in our demography are seen as having developed.

THE DEMOGRAPHIC REVOLUTION OF THE 1980S

The two key elements of the demographic revolution that has taken place since the end of the 1970s have been a huge reduction in the number of people marrying and having children in their 20s – which reflects some kind of combination of postponement and abandonment of marriage – and a sharp and continuing rise in the number and proportion of non-marital births.

A further recent element has been a cessation, for the moment at least, of the post-1980 decline in the number of marital births, which by 1995 had virtually halved, falling from over 70,000 to just under 38,000. In mid-1996 the number of such marital births levelled off and then rose slightly in 1997, by about 1.5%, remaining more or less stable thereafter at this slightly higher level.

TABLE 1

Births 1965-1998 (Thousands)

		1965	1980	1995	1998
Marital	First	13.6	18.5	11.0	11.6
	Other	48.5	51.9	26.9	26.8
	Total	62.1	70.3	37.9	38.4
Non-Marital	First	1.3	3.1	6.7	9.4
	Other	0.1	0.6	4.1	5.8
	Total	1.4	3.7	10.9	15.1
Total	First	14.9	21.6	17.8	21.0
	Other	48.6	52.5	31.0	32.6
Total		63.5	74.1	48.8	53.6

This recent phenomenon has been the product of an increase in first marital births to women aged 27 and over, which, since 1995, has much more than offset a further 22% drop in first marital births to women under 27. Within this recent period there has been an increase of over 20% in first births to married women aged 30-34 – and of almost 30% in first births to married women aged 35-39. This provides clear evidence of the 'biological clock' phenomenon – which is currently pushing many first pregnancies well beyond an optimum age.

TABLE 2

First Marital Births – Age of Mother 1965-1998 (Thousands)

Age of Mother	1965	1980	1995	1998
15-26	8.2	12.4	2.8	2.2
27-29	2.3	3.2	3.3	3.4
30-34	2.0	2.0	3.8	4.6
35-39	0.8	0.5	1.0	1.3
40 Upwards	0.2	0.1	0.2	0.2
Total (Incl. Not Stated)	13.6	18.5	11.0	11.6

a. Postponement and abandonment of marriage

The decline in the marriage rate between 1981 and 1998 was such that the married proportion of the 15-29 age-group, which had risen from 22% to 32% between 1961 and 1981, has since fallen to 13%. And, whereas in 1981 almost one-third of women aged 20-24 were already married, by the late 1990s this proportion had fallen as low as 5%.

TABLE 3

Marital Status of Women Aged 15-39, 1965-1998 (Thousands)

Age Group		1961	1981	1996	1998
15-29	Single	205.9	282.8	375.7	399.5
	Ever-married	58.4	134.2	63.8	59.4
	Total	264.2	417.1	439.5	458.8
30-39	Single	43.0	27.1	56.2	54.8
	Ever-Married	119.7	181.1	206.5	211.8
	Total	162.7	208.2	262.7	266.6

It is not clear to what extent these radical changes in Irish marriage practice have reflected merely a postponement of marriage or represent an actual abandonment of this institution.

Clearly a significant element of postponement is involved. This is reflected in the fact that while in the eleven-year period between 1984 and 1995 the proportion of marriages that involve women at ages under 25 fell by almost 65%, the proportion involving women aged 26-35 rose during this period by almost 70%. Moreover, of its nature postponement of marriage must involve an initial quite prolonged drop in the marriage rate, followed in time by a recovery, as those concerned finally take the plunge, and there may, therefore, be some significance in the fact that following a 28% drop in the number of marriages between March 1980 and March 1998, this figure recovered by as much as 10% in the twelve moths ended March 1999.

This trend towards much later marriages has also been reflected in the figures for marital births. Since 1984 the proportion of such births to women aged 23-26 has fallen from 23% to 15% while the proportion of births to women aged 31-35 has risen from 24% to 37%.

It should be said that for some time past this trend towards later marriages and births has been almost universal in Europe. Up to the mid-1970s contraception had been reducing the birth rates for women over 35 throughout Europe, but from the mid-1970s onwards in Scandinavia and Britain, and since the late 1980s in most other EU countries including Ireland, the mean age at child-bearing has been rising. By 1995 the birth rate for the 35-39 age group in some countries had actually doubled.

Where Ireland is unique, however, is in the fact that, even at their lowest point in 1987, births to women over 35 were higher than anywhere else in the EU, and the subsequent increase in this rate has kept it above the level of any other EU country – to an extent that must surely be worrying from a health point of view.

There are also indications that for some proportion of the new generation in Ireland marriage is being abandoned rather than merely postponed. Thus, a notable feature of the increase in the number of non-marital births has been the exceptional rise in the number of such births to older mothers. Whereas in 1981 only 7% of non-marital births were to women in their 30s, by 1998 this proportion had risen to 17%. Moreover, the proportion of such births to women aged 25 to 29 doubled during this period, rising from 12% to 24%.

TABLE 4

Non-marital Births 1981-1998 (Thousands)

Age of Mother	1981		1998	
	No.	%	No.	%
Under 20	1.5	38%	3.0	20%
20-24	1.6	41%	5.7	38%
25-29	0.5	12%	3.6	24%
30-34	0.2	5%	1.8	12%
35-39	0.1	2%	0.8	5%
40 And Over	—	—	0.2	1%
Total	3.9		15.1	

Furthermore the proportion of second or later non-marital births to women over age 25 rose sharply during this period, from 38% to 58% – and while a first non-marital birth may often be the unintended result of a casual encounter, second and later births are more likely to take place within an established relationship.

In the absence of research into co-habitation in Ireland, it is not possible at present to assess the precise extent to which by the end of the 1990s it has become common for non-marital relationships not only to precede marriage but to be maintained without recourse to marriage even after the birth of a child. While in some cases where this happens an undissolved marriage of one or other of the partners could account for this situation, in other cases it must presumably reflect an actual parental preference for an unrecognised union instead of marriage.

It is even more difficult to get a fix on the number of people who now choose initially to co-habit with a view to marrying when, whether by intent or otherwise, they later become parents. Nor do we know anything about the proportion who engage in casual pre-marital sex unrelated to co-habitation.

b. Rise in non-marital pregnancies

What we do know is that in the past two decades there has been an explosion in the number of non-marital births. Since 1981 the number of non-marital births has almost quadrupled from just under 4,000 to over 15,000 in 1998. Non-marital births now constitute 28% of all births, and almost 40% of first births. Given that 88% of Irish abortions in England and Wales involve single women, and that only 8%-10% are second abortions,[1] it is clear that the

1. Niamh Flanagan and Valerie Richardson, p. 30, *Unmarried Mothers: A Social Profile*, Dept. of Social Work /Social Science Research Centre, UCD, & Social Work Research Unit, Holles Street Hospital, 1992. (Also Green Paper On Abortion, September 1999, par. 6.07.)

proportion of pregnancies that are non-marital is now one-third, and just over half of all first pregnancies are now non-marital. Finally, over 35% of first non-marital pregnancies are now aborted in England or Wales.

TABLE 5
Irish Births and Abortions 1998 (Thousands)

	Marital	Non-Marital	Total
Total Births	38.4	15.1	53.6
Abortions*	.7#	5.2#	5.9
Total Pregnancies	39.1	20.3	59.4
Percentage Aborted	1.8%	25.5%	9.9%
First Births	11.2	8.0	20.2
Abortions*	.6^	4.7^	5.4^
Total Pregnancies	11.9	12.7	24.6
Percentage Aborted	5.4%	37.2%	21.4%
Other Births	27.2	7.1	34.3
Abortions*	.1	.5	.5
Total Pregnancies	27.3	7.6	34.9
Percentage Aborted	.2%	6.1%	1.5%

*Abortions in England and Wales to women giving addresses in the Irish State.
These figures are based on the fact that in 1996 only 11.9% of these abortions were to married women. (Green Paper on Abortion, Sept. 1999, Appendix 2, Table 2.)
^ 90%-92% of abortions are first abortions (Green Paper, par. 6.07). For the purpose of this Table it is assumed that in 1998 91% of both marital and non-marital abortions were first abortions.

All these figures ignore the possibility of under-statement of abortions in England and Wales to Irish residents, some of whom may give British addresses, as well as leaving out of account abortions to Irish residents in Scotland or Continental countries.

In interpreting these figures account must, however, be taken of several factors. First, there has been the impact of the post-1960 rise in the birth rate and the drop in emigration upon the number of young people in their 20s. And, second, there has been the decline in marriage amongst that age group. In combination these factors have contributed to an increase since 1981 of almost 50% in the number of single young people. Consequently the virtual quadrupling of non-marital births since that year has involved a two-and-half times increase in, rather than a quadrupling of, the ratio of non-marital births to the number of single young people. In 1998 the 15,000 non-marital births involved 3.25 births per 100 single women in the 15-39 age cohort, and the pregnancy rate for this cohort was 4.35 per 100.

Only the three Scandinavian EU members, with Britain, France and Austria appear to have higher proportions of non-marital births than Ireland.

However, because of the phenomenon of cross-border abortions, as well as uncertainty as to the proportion of abortions that are marital in different countries, international comparisons of the proportion of non-marital *pregnancies* are difficult. Nevertheless, although abortion rates are higher for women in many other countries than for Irish women, it is doubtful if the inclusion of this abortion factor would bring the non-marital pregnancy rate of the other eight EU countries above our figure.

Finally, it should perhaps be noted that there is evidence that a significant proportion of single mothers are in a stable relationship with the natural father at the time of the birth: 50% in the case of non-marital births in Holles Street Hospital in the years 1986-1989.[2] Moreover the Irish experience has been that one-quarter of natural fathers spend some of each day with their child, while over half of such fathers share some of the parenting role with the mother – two-thirds of whom are living with their former family a year later.[3] And many women with non-marital children remain in a stable relationship with the father, or subsequently marry – as may be seen from the fact that despite the temptation to deny co-habitation because of the Social Welfare provision for lone parents, claims by mothers for lone parent allowances in 1996 related to only 80,000 children – despite the fact that there had been 120,000 non-marital births in the preceding sixteen years.

c. Marriage breakdown and divorce

It is well-known that marriage breakdowns are increasingly common. The 1996 Census showed that 9% of couples within the age range 33-42 – the cohort most affected by the rising trend of marriage breakdown – were separated in that year, which represented an increase of three percentage points by comparison with the separation rate for this group five years earlier.

These figures also show that at every age level the increase in the proportion of separated couples in this most recent quinquennium was greater than in the immediately preceding quinquennium. If, as seems likely, this increase in the separation rate for each cohort continues in the future, the eventual cumulative separation rate for the younger married couples of today could be as high as one-third. And, even if the separation rate for each age cohort were to stabilise at its 1991-1996 level, the eventual Irish separation rate would exceed one-quarter.

This does not, however, imply a similar divorce rate: many separations do not end in divorce. At the time of the divorce referendum, I expressed the view that the Irish divorce rate would probably end up in the range 15-20%

---

2. Flanagan and Richardson, p. 30, op. cit.
3. Valerie Richardson, pp. 77 & 82, *In And Out of Marriage*, Family Studies Centre UCD, 1992.

– a good deal higher than in Italy, and perhaps somewhat higher than in Spain, but somewhat lower than the divorce rate for Catholics in Northern Ireland, and barely one-third of the British rate. With divorces granted during the legal year 1998/99 likely to number around 2,000, (a ratio of 12% to the number of marriages in that period), the gradual processing of the backlog of divorce cases seems likely to validate the 15%-20% forecast within the next couple of years. It may be worth noting, incidentally, that the number of legal separations has fallen by two-fifths since the introduction of divorce.

FACTORS CONTRIBUTING TO THESE SOCIAL CHANGES

Such are the basic facts about the changes that have taken place in social mores during the 1980s and 1990s. The picture is disturbing in several respects. The speed with which such huge changes have taken place in a society that had for long been stable, to the point of being in some respects unhealthily stagnant, has been quite extraordinary. It is difficult indeed to think of any other country within which so many and so great social changes have occurred within such a short period.

Clearly, against a background of changing mores throughout the industrial world as a whole, the sudden shift from economic stagnation in Ireland forty years ago to quite rapid economic growth set forces in motion underneath the surface of our society the effects of which became evident only after a delay of several decades. As late as 1981, twenty years after the start of this growth cycle, most people still saw the social effects of the preceding period of economic growth in a positive light.

For, the marriage boom and the increase in the birth rate that had marked the two preceding decades seemed at that time to offer a positive prospect of social stability combined with a renewed social dynamic – while a rise in non-marital births and the emergence of a significant level of Irish abortions in Britain had not yet attracted much attention. For my own part, I recall the exhilaration I experienced at the crowds of young couples with their families that thronged the streets as I campaigned in the June 1981 Election, which seemed to bode well for the future of our society.

What have been the precipitating elements in the process of radical social change which, starting imperceptibly in the 1970s, became increasingly apparent as we moved through the 1980s? Although there are several specifically Irish aspects, most of the forces at work have been operating in all industrial societies over many decades. In the Irish case they simply started later than elsewhere and were compressed into a shorter period. There were, however, several specifically Irish factors.

It appears to me that these factors can be summarised under six main headings: the growth of individualism, the much wider use of contraception, the expansion of female employment, the rapid increase in the level of education attained by young women, the decline in religious belief and practice, and the actual reversal of social pressures that previously operated against acceptance of pre-marital sex.

a. The growth of individualism

First, and perhaps most fundamental, has been the growth of individualism in Western society.

The culture of earlier periods was marked by, and required for its survival, strong social constraints: individuals had to conform to social norms, and there were limited opportunities for pursuing personal goals. Christian teaching blended respect for the individual, made in the image of God, with a strong social ethic that was designed to ensure the stability of society and, even more fundamental, the successful survival of the human race. Under conditions in which a high proportion of children failed to survive to maturity, this latter objective could be achieved only by unconstrained procreation within the shelter of a two-parent nuclear family.

During the nineteenth and twentieth centuries, humanity increasingly came to master its environment, and some of the social constraints previously needed for human survival thus became less necessary, leaving room for the development of an individualism which has expressed itself through, and in turn has been intensified by, the rapid development of the market system, of urbanisation, and of capitalism.

At the level of the family, child-bearing – which had previously been such an inevitable consequence of marriage for all but a small infertile proportion of couples – ceased to be inevitable, and, with much improved health conditions, could without risk to human survival be constrained. Indeed the risk to human survival shifted rapidly from a danger of too few children to a danger of too many – viz. over-population. This radical and almost overnight change in the evolutionary conditions of the human race undermined the rationale of the social constraints within which it had hitherto had to operate, and opened up a much wider range of human choices than heretofore. And this in turn paved the way for the release of an individualism which, until and unless constrained by modified social norms appropriate to this changed human condition, is proving to have a socially destructive potential.

b. Contraception

In the second place, an associated development which greatly enlarged the scope for uninhibited individualism has been the emergence and wide availability of forms of contraception. On the one hand this has provided parents with a means of limiting family size to compensate for the huge increase in child survival rates, while also making it possible for women to avoid late pregnancies, which are both dangerous for them and are more liable to produce children with mental or physical defects. At the same time, contraception has weakened greatly the constraints on extra-marital sexual relations, thus removing what had formerly provided an incentive to early marriage.

One of the effects of these developments seems to have been a significant shift in motivation amongst young people, involving a new emphasis on self-fulfilment at the expense of fulfilment through procreation. 'Child-bearing is becoming a transient rather than a central activity for many parents.'[4] The priority previously accorded to having children and successfully raising them has been replaced by a priority in favour of what is seen as the achievement of personal happiness. The rapid growth of marriage breakdown has derived largely from this aspect of individualism.

Associated with this individualist factor has been the emergence of a reluctance by young people to commit themselves to the kind of long-term relationship that is involved in marriage. This is an understandable reaction in the case of children of broken, or troubled, marriages but, to what appears a puzzling extent, it seems to be shared by most children of successful marriages, who in the past would have been encouraged by their parents' example to find a life-partner early in their own lives. The explanation sometimes given for this – that it is due to concerns with the increase in the average lifespan – is unconvincing, because the scale of this increase within the short period during which young people in Ireland have 'de-committed' – viz. the last twenty years – has been much too small to have had such an impact.

c. Movement of women into the labour force
The third factor contributing to radical changes affecting the family has been the movement into the labour force of a proportion of women who had previously worked in the home. This has relieved frustrations which many, albeit not all, women had previously felt at being house-bound.

The urge on the part of women to self-fulfilment through employment outside the home has also been facilitated by wider availability and use of contraception, which can secure either the earlier termination of child-bearing or postponement of the initiation of this process. Initially it was used by women primarily for the former purpose – more at first on health grounds than with a view to resuming employment – but latterly it has been employed mainly with a view to initiating, maintaining, and prolonging a career, through the postponement of child-bearing – and, indeed, of marriage.

---

4. Claire Carney, p. 48, *In And Out Of Marriage,* Family Studies Centre UCD, 1992.

Delays in the family initiation process have, however, failed to resolve the tensions inherent in women's dual capacity as bearers and early nurturers of children and also as members of the labour force. This problem may be particularly acute in Ireland where, to a greater extent than elsewhere, the increase in the number of young women in the labour force has reflected fulltime employment – and where, in the 1980s at any rate, husbands of employed women spent only four more hours a week in housework than husbands of women engaged fulltime in the home.[5]

It should, perhaps, be added that, because of the lesser provision of childcare in Ireland, lone mothers here are less likely to be employed than in other EU countries.[6]

The resolution of these tensions has not been helped by the fact that the pattern of work outside the home that had been evolved by men over centuries has not proved suitable, and has not been adapted, to the needs of those women who are endeavouring to fulfil this demanding dual role. The failure to accommodate our system of work to the fuller participation of women in the workforce, and more generally the failure of men to adjust their roles in the home to the new gender equality situation, are certainly factors that have aggravated the marriage breakdown factor

d. Impact of increased educational levels

There is a clear correlation between the educational level attained by women and the postponement of marriage and childbirth. The rapid rise in Irish educational attainment in recent decades has thus been a significant factor in the shift towards later marriages and first births.

e. Decline in religious belief and practice

A fifth factor in the changes that have been taking place in relation to the family has been the decline in religious belief and practice. Thus there is evidence that in Ireland marriage breakdown is more common amongst people with no religious affiliation.[7]

In many other industrialised countries this process began several centuries ago and was well-advanced by the time social changes affecting the family began to emerge. In Ireland, however, these two processes have effectively coincided – squeezing into the same quarter of a century developments that in countries like Britain and France were spread sequentially over two centuries. This specifically Irish aspect of the matter has not, I think, been widely enough recognised.

---

6. Valerie Richardson, pp.133 & 137, *Irish Family Studies*, Family Studies Centre UCD, 1995.
7. Máire Nic Ghiolla Phádraig, p.10, *In And Out Of Marriage*, Family Studies Centre UCD, 1992.

In this country there has in fact been something of a backlash against the conservatism of the institutional Catholic Church, which in the past acted as some kind of dam behind which, during the third quarter of the twentieth century, pressure for change built up on a scale that could not forever be denied. When that dam eventually burst in the final quarter of this century, this led eventually to something like a storm flood.

However apt or otherwise that storm flood analogy may be, what is now clear is that Irish society had previously been relying on a purely religious ethic, the rational basis of which had been fatally underplayed. When, for one reason or another, the religious authority behind what, to a much larger degree than most people realised, had come to be seen as an externally imposed set of values, evaporated, many young people, and some older ones, found nothing solid left to hang on to.

They had generally been left in ignorance of the fact that most of the church's moral teaching corresponded to a rational ethic, solidly founded on the needs of society. The gap left by the absence of a distinct but closely linked civic ethic, which would have provided a firm basis for such societal institutions as marriage, has since proved very damaging indeed.

Moreover, however paradoxical it may seem, the delay in the introduction of civil divorce may also have contributed to the undermining of marriage. For, in the absence of divorce, marriage breakdowns during the 1970s and early 1980s led increasingly to the formation of informal unions on a scale that soon led to a ready acceptance of such arrangements as normal elements in society. It was concern at the way in which marriage was thus being marginalised, in a manner damaging to social stability, that led me as Taoiseach to initiate the divorce referendum of 1986.

However, neither side in that debate proved willing even to address this key issue. The institutional church chose to campaign on the basis of simplistic and unverified sociological assertions, bolstered up by a dubious 'floodgate theory', which was sometimes combined with theological statements of a kind that were irrelevant to the issue of civil divorce. And these church spokesmen were backed by lay advocates who deployed emotive arguments about property, designed to frighten those who owned assets of various kinds, especially land.

Meanwhile, on the other side, most of the advocates of divorce were largely content to make a specious claim that something called a civic right existed to repudiate marriage contracts that had been entered into on the basis of indissolubility – backing this claim up with hard cases of the kind that make bad law.

There was simply no willingness to address the attempts I made to initiate a serious debate on whether we had or had not reached the stage at which the absence of any kind of divorce was creating a society in which the prolif-eration of unrecognised unions was undermining marriage to a greater extent than the availability of divorce was likely to do. While I recognise, of course, that the evaluation of the merits of this argument was, and remains, neces-sarily a matter of judgement, I have to say that the way events developed since 1986 has strengthened my belief that in the interest of social stability divorce should have been introduced a good deal earlier – probably in the late 1970s.

f. Social pressures against marriage

To the five factors just mentioned one other should perhaps be added. Just as in the past social pressures and example helped to maintain the older pat-tern of marriage and child-bearing, as well as rejection of pre-marital sex, such pressures and example now operate in the opposite direction. Those who have adopted a lifestyle that includes pre-marital sexual activity and postponement or abandonment of marriage are often motivated to justify this by creating social pressures favouring this new way of life. Young people, who are strongly influenced by peer pressures, then find it difficult to resist such a prevalent climate of opinion within their own generation.

POSSIBILITY OF ACTION TO SUSTAIN MARRIAGE

The range and scale of the pressures that now operate against marriage, and which favour late marital child-bearing, is such that it is not easy to see what effective measures can be taken to counter them. Moreover, the climate of social opinion is predominantly hostile to 'judgmental' interventions that favour one lifestyle as against another. Indeed, sociologists point to the often perverse effects of past judgmentalist approaches – for example, the impact of judgmentalist attitudes to non-marital births upon the tolerance of, and growing resort to, abortion by Irish young people in and after the 1970s.

However, these considerations have somewhat less force in today's per-missive climate and, while the case for caution in respect of interventions designed to influence social mores is a strong one, it would be wrong to rule out consideration being given to steps that might improve the working of our society. Only very dogmatic liberals would absolutely oppose any such inter-vention.

The problem is to devise actions that would help to reduce promiscuity, strengthen the stability of marriage, and reduce the pressures that are cur-rently pushing ever-later the initiation of families – but which would not at the same time prove counter-productive or have negative side-effects.

a. Paid parental leave

One measure which would not be contested socially, and which would certainly alleviate pressures favouring late initiation of families, would be the introduction of paid parental leave in Ireland. (In the EU only Ireland, Britain and Luxembourg lack this provision.) This might encourage many working wives to bring forward their first pregnancy to a much earlier date, to the advantage of both mothers and babies. There would, no doubt, be strong pressure against such a move from business sources – all the more so because of the current almost unique Irish labour shortage. Nevertheless the longer-term good of our society favours such a move.

b. Childcare facilities

The provision or subsidisation by the state of childcare facilities, if accompanied by parallel measures to assist non-labour force parents caring for their children at home, would also help, as would much more generous Child Allowance provisions. Despite recent improvements, our Child Allowance provisions remain less generous than anywhere else in the EU outside the Iberian peninsula.

c. Measures to encourage marriage

It would certainly be desirable that positive disincentives to marriage in our income transfer system – income tax and social welfare – be eliminated.

Examples of the extent to which our present system discourages lone parents from marrying are given in Chapter 11 of the *Report Of The Working Group Examining The Treatment of Married, Co-habiting, And One-Parent Famliies Under The Tax And Social Welfare Codes* (September 1999). In such cases income losses of up to 35% can arise through marriage – or, of course, through an admission of co-habitation. The Working Group has offered five options designed to remedy, individually or in combination, these negative features of our existing transfer system.

A more difficult area is the provision of direct incentives for marriage. Opposition to this would come from those who would see this as involving a judgmentalism that would reflect negatively on people who for one reason or another are in unrecognised unions. To this objection there are several possible responses.

First of all, the widespread social acceptance of such unions today, and the fact that they are no longer effectively forced on some couples by the absence of divorce, have weakened the anti-judgmental argument. Moreover, there is, I believe, a real difference between on the one hand positively discriminating against unrecognised unions – which is still a feature of our Constitution and of some of our legislation – and on the other hand positively encouraging marriage – an institution which the state, on behalf of society, has a legitimate interest in encouraging.

A bigger difficulty is that artificial incentives may achieve not merely the purpose they are designed to achieve – they may also have unintended negative effects. Thus, incentives for marriage might over-persuade some couples who are ill-suited to entering upon a permanent relationship, and thus eventually increase the marriage breakdown problem.

Nevertheless, given the scale of postponement and abandonment of marriage in Ireland today, the idea of some kind of incentives for marriage should not be dismissed out of hand.

More generally, in the general social interest the case for more intensified relationship education is a strong one. Many of our family problems today are not due to inherent parental character defects but to lack of early preparation for this aspect of life – something that many parents clearly have difficulty about offering to their children. Leaving these matters to the much later stage of pre-marriage courses is irresponsible. In many cases attitudes and habits have already been formed long before that point is reached.

d. A challenge for the churches

The churches as well as the state have a role to play here, given that the vast majority of children still attend church schools. This responsibility has not always been exercised sensibly or effectively.

On the one hand, when, as often happens during the late stages of childhood, religious authority is rejected, an earlier failure to establish in the minds of the children in question that basic Christian teaching on issues related to marriage is founded on a rational appreciation of human needs, opens the way to irresponsible behaviour. Reason is not a dangerous rival to religion: in areas like this it can instead provide a badly needed re-inforcement of religious teaching.

Next, to the extent that the credibility of the Catholic Church's basic stance on marriage is undermined by some late accretions to that church's teaching – such as the invalidity (as distinct from illicit nature) of non-Catholic marriages of Catholics, the Pauline and Petrine privileges, and the bigamous re-marriage of some undivorced partners to annulled marriages, (the latter of which seems to be a peculiarly Irish phenomenon) – these should be reviewed, if the church wishes to recover its moral authority in these areas.

But the biggest obstacle in the way of the Catholic Church being able to recover credibility in these matters remains the rejection by Pope Paul VI of the majority view of the church's Commission on Contraception. That contraception can be – is indeed certain to be – abused by many is no more a reason for banning it than drunkenness is a reason for declaring the consumption of alcohol to be a mortal sin. And the alternative approach of attempting to make a fundamental moral distinction between 'natural' and 'artificial' contraception is not merely unconvincing but is the kind of thing that gives theology a bad name.

It is probably the case that until this mistake has been retrieved – if that be possible – the capacity of the Catholic Church to offer persuasive leadership in matters sexual will remain negligible.

CONCLUSION

As in Britain, intellectual life in Ireland has been predominantly literary, rather than philosophical and political. In these islands we seem to lack the wider intellectual interest in social and philosophical issues which has been such a characteristic of French society. At a time of such rapid social change, this is a serious deficiency.

There is a most disturbing absence of informed debate about the many recent developments which affect marriage in our society in a most fundamental way.

First of all, public awareness of demographic changes in our society lags far behind the reality: we are living in a society that is now quite different from the one we have been accustomed to in the quite recent past, and most people are only dimly aware of or, to the extent that they are so aware, greatly underestimate the scale and significance of the changes that have taken place in social behaviour.

Second, such discussion as has taken place on these issues has tended to be simplistically polarised between rather inarticulate conservative voices on the one hand and highly vocal liberal and sometimes extreme feminist writers and speakers on the other. This type of polarisation, beloved of the media, and especially of television, kills serious debate.

Thirdly, there does not seem to be any forum in which such a serious debate can be effectively organised. There is, of course, much discussion of social policy amongst professional sociologists, who through their research and publications are making a major contribution to our knowledge of aspects of these problems. But the wider community – including many opinion-formers, and people who ought to be opinion-formers – is not involved in this internal professional process, and is often unaware of many of the issues at stake.

It is time that we faced up to these deficiencies in our intellectual life.

The Media and the Enemies of Truth

John Horgan

In the autumn of 1967, in a high-ceilinged meeting room tucked away behind the Via della Conciliazione in Rome, a protest meeting was taking place. The room itself was something out of the ordinary: it was a Moravian place of worship, established at the heart of the Roman Catholic empire as part of the Moravian missionary outreach. The slogan emblazoned on the wall – fittingly, in Latin – said it all: *Lux lucebit in tenebris.*

The meeting was protesting at the new arrangements for media information set in place by the Vatican Press Office – then, as frequently, an oxymoron – for the first Synod of Bishops. Two years earlier, the media had departed Rome after seeing the culture of clerical secrecy and obfuscation, which had attended the opening of Vatican II, give way – not without a struggle – to a degree of openness and transparency that few could have predicted. Now, two years down the road, it appeared that the stone had been rolled back in front of the cave. The shutters were down, and the official view seemed to echo that famously expressed by a US senator on the role of the state *vis-à-vis* war correspondents: 'I wouldn't tell them anything until after it was over. Then I'd tell them who won.'

The chief speaker at the meeting was the diminutive Dominican theologian, Fr Chenu. What he lacked in stature he made up for in presence. He seemed almost to levitate as he exclaimed, with passion: *'Tout blocâge de communication est un péché contre le Saint Esprit!'*[1]

The Holy Spirit is the spirit of truth (Jn 16:5-15). Inside the church or outside it, he is the test by which the efficacy of communication can best be tested. Even in the secular world, truth is a concept which has weight, although it may not have a specifically Christian or religious dimension. It is a concept which journalists and the media, above all, have an interest in identifying and defending against its enemies and even – perhaps especially – against those who claim to have a monopoly of it.

When Christians take the witness stand in a court of law, they promise under oath to tell 'the truth, the whole truth, and nothing but the truth'.

---

1. Roughly, 'Every obstacle placed in the way of communication is a sin against the Holy Spirit.'

Earning one's crust as a journalist involves no such weighty undertakings; and yet journalists generally would be highly affronted if they were accused of being untruthful. Such errors as appear in their work, they will argue, arise from any one of – or a combination of – factors largely outside their control. Other people tell them lies, which they publish in good faith. Honest mistakes are made. The pressure of time produces compression and distortion.

All of these arguments are valid some of the time. None of them is valid all the time. Now, as the century turns, it is appropriate for journalists to take some time for reflection, to identify the enemies of truth, and to sketch out some strategies designed to counter them, or at least to minimise the dangers they pose. The list suggested in this article is by no means exhaustive – in a sense it is only a list of headlines – and is intended as a staging post in the journey of exploration and moral discovery which, for journalists concerned about the validity of their work, never really ends.

The impact of technology

The age in which we live is marked, not least as the media are concerned, by two characteristics in particular. One is the increasing importance of technology. The other is the post-modernist paradigm in which all the priesthoods, all the hierarchies, are crumbling and evaporating, and values, ideologies and structures are increasingly mixed up in a sort of great, primordial soup.

Technology itself is ambiguous – sometimes an enemy of the truth, sometimes its friend. We have only to look at the contest between journalism and governments in relation to the Balkans in recent months, for example, to realise that technology offers new possibilities for the reporting of conflict, and to predict that relationships between journalists and governments will become more uncomfortable than ever before. The journalism of this and other conflicts, aided and abetted by new technology, at one level has the potential to free people from the silken threads of the conspiracies sometimes woven by their rulers.

The theory of the just war, when it was first elaborated, was discussed between theologians who had rarely even seen a bow and arrow fired in anger, and in an atmosphere of arcane inquiry far removed from the events to which it related. Today, people make up their minds about the morality of what is going on in the light of the evidence offered by journalists on their television screens, several times a day. The moral landscape is shifting and changing before our eyes, and we have the opportunity to evaluate it as never before, thanks to the conjunction, on occasion, of traditional journalistic skills and the new technologies.

This is why governments now realise that the media's role in shaping public attitude to war cannot any more be taken for granted, and why they react in such a Pavlovian fashion to inconvenient disclosures, at the same time as they refine their own techniques of disinformation and manipulation.

But the new technologies are not necessarily value-free, or neutral. They are generally developed, distributed and used by organisations that produce news and information primarily as a commodity whose shelf-life is often more important than its content. At worst, the technology is structurally subservient to that other marketing imperative of the modern media – not selling news, but selling viewers, listeners and readers to advertisers.

What the new technology offers is immediacy, not necessarily meaning. It seems to offer everyone the possibility of being an eye-witness at everything; but the perspective it offers is, in truth, very partial. It does not do away with the need for journalists, as is sometimes supposed: but it changes the nature of their job in ways that we have not yet fully explored.

We can be with the NATO troops as they roll into Kosovo, but does this explain the war? We can be a fly on the wall as George Bush Jr launches his presidential campaign, but will we know who's paying his bills? We can print our newspapers in all the colours of the rainbow, but will this only serve to obscure the fact that the truth is best read in black and white? The new technology will allow journalists to tell us what they think with hitherto unparalleled frequency and strength: but will it let us talk back to them?

The siren song of the new technology for journalists is this: I have it first, therefore I have it best. But is first always best? And the speed with which information can travel in today's world, and the technology which is used to transmit it, will, unless we take steps to control it, reduce many journalists to the role of processors, rather than originators of information, information which serves sectional interests rather than the public interest.

If the new technology, among other things, makes journalism theoretically more powerful than ever before, the other side of the paradox is that some journalists do not use this power at their disposal at all. More than two decades ago, a seminal study of the *New York Times*[2] found that close to half of the information it offered its readers as 'news' was attributed to US government officials, and another 27% to 'foreign officials'. Only 1% of all news stories were based on the reporter's own observation and analysis. It would be nice to think that things have changed. Somehow I doubt it. One of the tasks of journalism today is precisely to identify and analyse the ways in which the sophistication and power potentially at the command of modern journalists

2. *News, The Politics of Illusion*, by W. Lance Bennett, New York, Longman, 1983.

can be harnessed in the interests of truth, and not merely exploited in the pursuit of profit. It needs to be harnessed, if we are to deal effectively with the challenge posed by the increasingly sophisticated and self-interested publicity systems which still provide most of what we misleadingly dignify with the title 'news'.

Journalists are still slow to recognise this as a real challenge, and to do something about it. For the most part, they tend to concentrate on other, more obvious external enemies of truth. In the past, and still to some extent today, the chief of these is censorship.

We still have an Official Secrets Act, although it sits increasingly uncomfortably beside the Freedom of Information Act on the statute book. The censorship embodied in the Broadcasting Acts is still in existence, although it has been suspended for the time being. The Offences Against the State Act (now belatedly the subject of review by a parliamentary committee) has provisions which are at least potentially draconian for the media, as do the Defence Acts. In many countries other than Ireland, the situation is often far worse: in a few, it is better.

Information overload

The main current external enemy of truth, however, is probably not censorship as such, but – paradoxically – information. There has never been as much information available, and about so many institutions, individuals and subjects. The problem is that, for the most part, it is genetically modified information – a commodity which excites only a fraction of the concern devoted to genetically modified food, perhaps because it is so useful to so many people. From the Internet, from government press offices, from off-the-record briefings, from high-powered public affairs consultancies and more lowly public relations offices, from pressure groups, lobby organisations, and lunatics, comes an unending flood of facts, comments, views, subtle hints and blatant propaganda.

In this context, the problem is not the absence of information but a superfluity, and the quality of it. The time for analysing and sifting this huge and exponentially increasing flow of information has not been extended proportionately. If anything, it has even been compressed by the demands of media competition, itself another insidious enemy of the truth. Even superhuman journalists would be hard-pressed to weigh all this additional information within a time horizon that is shrinking by the day – much less find the time for the sort of independent enquiry which is at the root of the best journalism, and is best calculated to serve the truth.

Under these circumstances, the temptation to accept the most likely story, to go with the flow, to accept the limitations with a shrug of the shoulders, is well-nigh overpowering. Journalists cannot fight it on their own, because the task of sifting the wheat from the chaff involves primarily time: and time is what their employers are most conscious of, because that means money. And in this context, those forms of media competition which put a higher priority on gossip, on personality journalism, on entertainment journalism, are as much enemies of truth as any form of state regulation or restriction.

And this underlines the importance of inculcating, in journalists, the sometimes dangerously atrophied skill of observation, and the ability to give a credible, accurate and even meaningful account of what has been observed. And this means, in turn, that newspaper and broadcast organisations will have to accept that the most fundamental form of investment they can make in pursuit of the truth is in journalists' time.

A new respect for time involves a re-birth of respect for an old-fashioned art: the art of reporting. One of my former mentors, asked once for a definition of the word 'journalist', paused for a moment before replying succinctly: 'A journalist is a reporter who's out of work.' But time is always in short supply; and the competition and profit-driven pressure on time remains a major enemy of truth in the media, but is one of which many journalists are still only dimly aware.

Libel laws and the protection of sources

As I have said, they tend to concentrate on the external enemies of the truth. As well as censorship, there are the libel laws. As well as the libel laws, there is the failure of the state to protect the confidentiality of journalists' sources. Without reform in these areas, we are told, the job of the courageous, crusading journalist is impossible, and truth is the ultimate casualty. Changing the ground rules, they argue, is a small price to pay for the flood of ground-breaking journalism which will ensure, for the cleansing of the Augean stables which is in prospect.

Of course the libel laws should be reformed – but not because they are bad for journalists (which they may be) but primarily because they are bad for society, and they are bad for society because they are inherently biased towards the rich and powerful, littered with anomalies, and a self-help gravy train for lawyers. But one of the worst things about them, ironically, is that they encourage, in the media, a sort of defeatism – the belief that good, honest reporting is incapable of circumventing the difficulties created by such laws, and is therefore rarely worth even attempting.

What about special protection for journalists' sources? At first this looks like a reasonably arguable case. It has been recognised in British law since 1981. The protection of sources is indeed a cardinal ethic of the profession, and there are undoubtedly many instances in which information of huge public importance will never see the light of day unless the informant can be guaranteed confidentiality. But does this mean, in turn, that the journalist should be up there on a pedestal with the doctor, the lawyer and the priest as one of the few authorised repositories of confidential information who has the right to protect its confidentiality?

I think not, and for three reasons. The first is that the analogies are suspect. The protection afforded to doctors, priests and lawyers is quite different from that sought by some journalists. Many people will know who the lawyer's client is, who is the doctor's patient, and – perhaps – even the identity of a penitent. It is the content of the communication, not the identity of the informant, which is primarily protected.

The law protects the content of these communications because it values highly the nature of the relationship. We as journalists are, as yet, a long way from proving that the quality of our relationships with our sources is of such importance and significance to society that the identity of our sources should be protected, while at the same time we trumpet our right to publish the content of what they have told us. The politics of concealing the identity of a source are quite different from the politics of concealing the content of a communication.

This brings me to the second reason. Journalists have a vested interest, not in concealment but in disclosure. We habitually refer to our work as 'stories'. But their are two elements to any story: one is the content, the other is the identity of the teller. Generally, we need to know the identity of the person telling the story before we can evaluate it properly, and check it out for special agendas, motives, and bias. Where the source remains confidential, there is a dangerous elision, an implication that journalist and story-teller are one and the same person.

In these circumstances, the further danger is that the journalist will come to see the source's interests and the interests of journalism as coterminous, and will end up in a self-justificatory *cul de sac*. What starts life as a working practice, a hand-hewn way of doing things which is justified by its results, is elevated into a principle which must be defended against all comers and in all circumstances, however dubious.

But there is a third reason. It is that journalists are also citizens. They are citizens before they become journalists, while they work as journalists, and after they cease being journalists. And citizenship is a higher calling even than journalism, despite the fact that it is much devalued in today's society.

The implications of this is that, faced with a dilemma about confidentiality, journalists should respond primarily as citizens. Does this mean that they will readily reveal their sources, and that no confidence will ever be observed? Of course not. For a start, the occasions on which disclosure of a journalist's confidential source is required for the proper administration of justice are few and far between. Prosecutors and judges alike shy away from putting journalists into the witness box unless it is absolutely necessary. Even when journalists have been summoned as witnesses, there have been comparatively few occasions on which their evidence has been decisive.

But when they do end up in the witness box, journalists face a problem which is not faced by the other professional groups I have mentioned, and do so without the same protections. What I am suggesting is that there may well be occasions, if this happens, when they will feel it necessary to protect their sources, but they ought to do so in the clear knowledge that, like Antigone, they will have to accept the consequences, come what may.

In the last resort, journalism is primarily a responsibility to be exercised by some citizens on behalf of the citizenry as a whole. If we come to regard it, instead, as a privilege to be defended, we will be in grave danger of aping other discredited hierarchies, in an age in which privilege is now often regarded more as a cloak for wrong-doing than as a legitimate social function.

Are journalists consistent, for example, in campaigning for freedom of information and relying so heavily on anonymous sources? To choose an example comfortably far from home, I can instance *The Guardian,* which is campaigning strongly against Jack Straw's ludicrous Freedom of Information Bill, but which sees no problem in publishing attacks on the new Poet Laureate which are fuelled by three conveniently anonymous sources.

The bottom line for journalism is that it is a contract, not with a source, but with the public, and we should never lose sight of that.

We may, however, be myopic if we give general currency to the idea that the enemies of truth are all external to the media. Are some of them at least partly internal? The internal ones are, I would argue, at least as important as the external ones, especially if they originate in a mistaken attempt to elevate the journalist into a new, almost hieratic role.

Internal enemies of truth

Journalists should be the last people to give themselves airs and graces. And we have only to look at what is happening in religion, in politics, even in law, to know that ancestral certainties, which indeed never really existed in any universal sense, are now no more.

The high Victorian model of an ordered world, with the rich man in his castle and the poor man at his gate, has long been consigned to the dustbin of history. The ancient priesthoods of religion and political power are crumbling before our eyes and, as they crumble, other priesthoods jostle to succeed them: those of the sociologists, the economists, and the technologists, to name only a few.

Where do journalists stand in all of this? I raise the question because of the need for journalists to resist the temptation to rush in and attempt to fill this vacuum of power, to resolve this crisis of legitimacy, on their own. If there is a power vacuum, we should be standing outside, watching who goes in, and what they do when they get there. We journalists should be warned against taking their place, if by nothing else, by the repeated findings of public attitude surveys that the level of public trust in our profession is, by and large, on a par with that of people who sell insurance door-to-door.

But there is another reason. It is because we journalists should be the last to believe our own press notices, our big by-lines, our journalism awards, and should be the first to remember that our profession is primarily one of service, not of domination, influence or control. I sometimes detect, in the campaigns that you will have noted from time to time for reform of the libel laws, and for the legal protection of journalists' sources, the kind of special pleading that is intimately bound up with a well-nourished sense of self-importance.

This can, at worst, engender a macho professionalism. Journalists who are – often rightly – critical of the arrogance of those in power can express their own criticisms with a lack of self-doubt which is in itself remarkable. They find it all too easy to slip from a culture of investigation, which is vital, into a culture of disparagement, which is more problematic. We should remember that while journalism is a necessary watchdog for democratic values and structures, it is not a substitute for them.

Frank Gallagher, first editor of the *Irish Press*, giving his instructions to his newly enlisted reporters and sub-editors in 1931, warned them, wisely: 'It is not necessary to report every word of praise spoken by judges to policemen.' But journalists have also to recognise that there are times when even policemen deserve praise.

Of course the watchdog function of journalism is a vital one, and if anything not sufficiently exercised in our society. But it is not the only function, and if we concentrate on it too much we will develop a sort of tunnel vision. I have warned against what might be described as the culture of disparagement – the idea that journalism is always oppositional, that those in power are never right. This culture of disparagement, with all its faults, is better than the culture of complicity. But journalism needs to find a working space between these two extremes. I hesitate to name it, but I know that it is there.

There are other features of the contemporary media which could equally be described as enemies of the truth. Let me itemise a few of them. There is, for example, the black art of 'water-cooler journalism', the tendency of journalists to agree privately among themselves what 'the story' is, which is at best a lazy way of doing your job, and at worst an outright fraud upon the public.

There is the temptation:

– to use the weasel words that slant their reports for or against the people or institutions they're writing about, while enabling the writer to escape the accusation of overt bias;

– to identify the soft targets which can be pilloried with impunity, while leaving the dangerous or powerful ones alone;

– to put their by-lines on top of re-written press releases (or even un-re-written press releases);

– to second-guess employers' and superiors' politics and prejudices so that they will rise, like helium-filled balloons, through the promotional structures of their organisations;

– to insulate themselves with layers of technology – email, the telephone, the VDU – from the real world they are supposed to be reporting on; and

– to flatter the rich and powerful with their attention so that they are welcomed into the mutual admiration society for which the only other essential entry requirement is the suspension of their critical faculties.

This is not, let me stress, a blanket accusation against Irish journalism. There are many, many Irish journalists who know these pitfalls of old, and who spend most of their working lives avoiding them, sometimes with little enough support from their superiors and employers.

The journalist's job is a difficult one at the best of times, and beset by many external threats and difficulties, which should not be underestimated. But the challenge by journalists to these external threats and difficulties will be immeasurably strengthened if it is accompanied by a sort of professional examination of conscience which, whether inspired by or related to religious convictions or not, is linked in some fundamental way to the pursuit of truth which is an inescapable dimension of the human condition.

The Good Friday Agreement:
A Christian Perspective

Gerry O'Hanlon

Introduction

The euphoria attending the Good Friday Agreement of 1998 has long since evaporated. However the possibility still remains that this Agreement may be the major catalyst of change in Irish society as we go forward into the next century. History will duly record whether this potential, appropriate to the hope which a new millennium conjures up, is eventually realised. What seems clear now, however, is that the Agreement needs all the help it can get to realise that potential. In this regard the contribution of the Christian churches will be of particular significance.

I propose to examine this contribution by means of a linked, three-step analysis. First, I address the vexed issue of the relationship between religion and politics. Next, I identify reconciliation as the key contribution which religion can offer to further the objectives of the Agreement. And finally I focus on the thorny issues surrounding the role of the central Christian sacrament of the eucharist as a symbol of reconciliation.

1. Religion and politics

It is of course by no means self-evident that the Christian churches can make a significant positive contribution to the reception and implementation of the Good Friday Agreement. It is well known that religion in many ways has been part of the problem rather than the solution in Northern Ireland. Too often religion and theology have tended to be both integralist and fundamentalist: that is to say, the link between the kingdom of God and political allegiance has been too close, and has been couched anachronistically in Reformation and counter-Reformation terms in order to reinforce the conflicting political identities and allegiances in Northern Ireland. One may refine this rather sweeping generalisation by reference to the nuances of political Protestantism and cultural Catholicism analysed in publications such as those of the Interchurch Group on Faith and Politics and in the 1997 text of the Department of Theological Questions of the Irish Inter-Church Meeting entitled *Freedom, Justice and Responsibility in Ireland Today*. However it is sufficient at this stage to have drawn attention to the problematic nature of the relationship between religion and politics. Nor is this problematic limited to Northern Ireland. The Republic of Ireland, along with many Western liberal democracies, is now struggling with is own perversion of the relationship between religion and politics, in that it is in danger of opting for a form of church-state separation which is exclusivist in so far as it relegates religion to the private sphere.

An historical note may help to clarify the nature of this relationship. Duncan Forrester[1] notes that in ancient society the state was understood to be part of a divine cosmic order such that piety and patriotism were virtually indistinguishable. Religious mythological ways of understanding the world were politically conservative in serving as a buttress for the state. This remained true of the civil religion in its classical form, found in the ancient Greek and Roman city-states. Religion did not seek to change the established order, rather it proclaimed that it was God-given and sacrosanct. However, there were some challenges to this worldview, from several sources. First, there was the beginning of a theory of natural law, which maintained that there were universal norms against which the laws and customs of each society may be judged. It is to these norms that Sophocles' Antigone appealed when deciding to bury her brother's body against the edict of Creon, the king of Thebes. Then there was the beginning of critical philosophy with Socrates, corrosive of the traditional political theology and civil religion. Finally there was that strand in Judaism, which while affirming that the social and political orders are created by God, nonetheless maintained that it does not derive from this fact any inherent sanctity. The prophets in particular make it clear that rulers are under God's will and law. They are always answerable to God, who is a God of justice, not of arbitrary power, a God who has special care for the poor and weak.

This critical moment is enhanced in Christianity where the preaching by Jesus of the kingdom of God may be understood to imply that the state is set free from religious control, while simultaneously it is cut down to size and deprived of its religious pretensions. This is so because the kingdom is open to all, transcending ethnic and particular political divisions, and so is in tension with narrower loyalties, including earthly citizenship. This means that in principle the preaching of the kingdom by Jesus secularised politics (give to Caesar ...), while affirming that the state and political activity are intimately related to God's purposes (in the confrontation with Pilate, Jesus is clear that Pilate's power comes 'from above', that Pilate is responsible to God). But for

---

1. For what follows, cf D. Forrester, *Theology and Politics,* Blackwell, Oxford, 1988.

different reasons, including the imminent expectation of the end-time and the fact that the early church was a minority sect, the New Testament does not contain more than fragments and hints of a political ethic.

Early Christianity was faced with the challenge of giving this new relationship between the religious and the political a theological interpretation. Forrester outlines three basic interpretative models which derive from this early period. First, with Tertullian (c.160-220), there is an anti-political separation of Christians from the doomed multitudes *(massa perditionis)* of the secular world. Within this model the church becomes a counter-culture to an alien and hostile state, without responsibility for power or any involvement in the world of politics. Despite the sectarian nature of this withdrawal from politics, this focus on an alternative society or counter-kingdom did in practice serve to challenge the political *status quo* and became a source of new ideas for Western political thought. Secondly, and at the other end of the spectrum, with Eusebius of Caesarea (264-340), there is the notion of Christianity as the new civil religion, a political theology in the classical mode suitable for the new relationship between church and empire which followed the Constantinian settlement. In this model the eschatological (already/not yet) character of Jesus' kingdom of God is almost submerged beneath the glory of present reality and there is massive sacral legitimation of the existing political order of things. The merit of this approach was to enhance stability and take seriously the duties of citizenship. Finally, around the centre of the spectrum, there is the towering figure of St Augustine (353-430). Critical of the Roman Empire, Augustine distinguished between the earthly city and the City of God. In the former, although the desire to dominate *(libido dominandi)* is characteristic, there may be a fragmented and partial peace and justice arising out of the balancing of claims and interests. This incomplete justice is a good necessary for stable social life, but it is not the highest good which can only be found in the divine justice and love of the City of God. The latter transcends the earthly city, but is relevant to both understanding and behaviour there. The church as it exists on earth is a mixed reality and cannot simply be identified with the City of God. However it can serve as a sign of God's city, and in witnessing to God's love is in contrast to the lust for glory and power that is characteristic of the *civitas terrena*. In so doing, it makes an immense contribution to the life of the polity, in setting goals, in denouncing abuses of power and in offering guidance. Secular politics then is taken seriously by Augustine; he affirms the theological significance of the political order and its need to be nourished and challenged by the gospel, but he relentlessly excludes it from the sphere of the sacred.

Once again, but in a less sectarian way than Tertullian, one notes an early pointer in the direction of the God-ordained secularity of politics, and yet the continuing relevance of a religious worldview.

Historically of course, through figures such as Aquinas, Luther and Calvin, and into the modern period, there has been a development of these three basic theological interpretative models. Our contemporary situation in most of the Western world leans towards the Tertullian model: modernity involves an increasing theological evacuation of the public realm. Northern Ireland may still represent a Eusebian exception to this prevailing norm. The challenge is to negotiate a middle-ground of critical dialogue and relative autonomy between the extremes of exclusivist separation (the tendency now in the Republic) and over-identification between religion and civil society (the North still, and the Republic also until quite recently). Perhaps this historical perspective frees us to imagine possible approaches to this challenge.

Would one such approach not have been a more straightforward recommendation of the Good Friday Agreement by the leaders of the Christian churches? Should the churches have told the people how to vote, and not just analysed the values at stake and urged them to exercise their vote? I suggest that given the recent historical context in both parts of Ireland, with the over-identification of religion and politics, it is entirely understandable that the churches refrained from a more direct endorsement of the Agreement. After all, even if, in the words of Seamus Heaney in the wake of the Good Friday Agreement, 'the Rev Ian Paisley and the Rev William McCrea of the DUP have tried to turn constituencies into congregations',[2] it is also true ironically that the influence of John Charles McQuaid on civil leaders lends some substance to Paisley's shibboleth that 'Home Rule is Rome Rule'. In this context Dr Patrick Hannon[3] is surely correct in noting that while Roman Catholics in particular are bound to give due weight to magisterial teaching on socio-political issues, the more particular and applied this teaching becomes, the less binding it is, the more it is susceptible to criteria of purely practical rationality, and the more open to a dissent that is not disloyalty. Hannon notes with approval how, from the 1970s on, the Roman Catholic Bishops have asserted the right and duty of legislators and citizens to make up their own minds on socio-political issues, while reserving their own right and duty to give guidance on such issues. This kind of guidance, motivated and formed by the biblical vision, will be most effective when given in an apt

---

2. *Irish Times*, Saturday, April 11, 1998.
3. For what follows, cf Patrick Hannon, *Church, State, Morality and Law*, Gill and Macmillan, Dublin, 1992.

teaching mode which seeks to persuade by appeal to reason, and which is non-authoritarian and non-paternalistic in style. There is a continuing role for all the churches in speaking out in this mode in the public realm in support of the objectives of the Good Friday Agreement.

2. Reconciliation as the key contribution of religion

The Agreement itself refers to the notion of reconciliation, while more recently in the Hillsborough Declaration of March 1999, there was a call for a reconciliation event to become part of the solution to the decommissioning impasse. In this context, we need an understanding of Christianity which invites us to move in the direction of the reconciliation of difference. This theology of reconciliation will not try to deny difference or ignore issues of justice: it will however be confident that difference and diversity may co-exist with unity (is this not what our central Christian paradigm of the Trinity of love is about?), and that justice within the Christian revelation is a necessary, but not sufficient, component of that love which reconciles. Such a theology will not presume to simply mirror the Good Friday Agreement, as if there were no specific differences between the realm of politics and that of religion. In particular, due attention will be given to a prudent assessment of the right time for acts of reconciliation in the secular, public sphere. But neither will secular and religious notions of reconciliation be regarded as simply belonging to separate spheres, as though a mutually sustaining dialogue were not possible.[4]

What might this dialogue challenge the churches to do differently? This is an important question, because the answer lies in the hands of Christians themselves. I suggest two related approaches to an answer. First, if it is true that the early narrative and preaching of the good news received its focus and theological colouring from the particular crisis situation which Paul and the evangelists found themselves addressing in different communities, then it is arguable that our living of Christianity in Northern Ireland today ought to focus on this reality of reconciliation. Everything should centre around this, our churches should mobilise their considerable forces with this end in view. Professor Terence Brown, having listened to the attempts by believers to tackle the situation in Northern Ireland, noted that 'I gained the sense that no church in Ireland has made peace and reconciliation in the country a driving,

---

4. For a further development of this theology of reconciliation, cf G. O'Hanlon, 'Reconciliation and Justice', in M. Hurley, ed, *Reconciliation in Church and Society,* Dublin, Institute of Irish Studies, 1994, pp 48-67.

determining imperative in its overall mission to society north and south.'[5] Of course it is not easy for church leaders, even if they wanted to, to simply mobilise their members around one basic option. In this context, Geraldine Smyth refers to a certain 'structural density and procedural deficit'[6] within churches which makes authoritative statements and actions difficult. But perhaps if there was more clarity of vision, a more effective way might be found to implement it. It is in this context that the importance and intelligibility of the following basic principle becomes apparent: 'when there is tension over important religious values then churches should opt for the interpretation which will enhance relationships in the interests of peace and reconciliation and ultimately of life itself'.[7] This principle does not ask us to compromise on truths which are central to our faith and which are securely held. Rather it applies to situations where there are different views validly held within any of our churches on controversial issues, asking us to opt for that view which best helps reconciliation, because reconciliation is important to Christ.

Secondly, why do the different churches not set up for themselves, in the manner most appropriate to their own character, a process whereby they undertake a thorough review of their pastoral strategy, in the light of the reality of the on-going sectarian divisions on our island and of the deep need for reconciliation? This review or audit, a kind of Pastoral Assembly of representatives of all the People of God within a particular church, should be with a view to turning around the respective ecclesial institutions in the direction of the reconciliation that is so urgently needed at different levels – ecumenically, culturally, politically, socially and economically. Of course assemblies on their own do not automatically guarantee change. Nonetheless, with clear terms of reference, careful preparation, a critically discerned process, and above all a strong determination to make a concerted attempt to turn things around decisively, one might reasonably hope for substantial achievement. If politicians are being asked to do this, why not also church people? Such an attempt at institutional conversion might be risky: but with the paradigm of evangelical dying and rising as its inspiration, is this really a risk which the churches can refuse to take, if they wish to remain churches of Jesus Christ?

A final comment on this second point, and a link with my third point. There is perhaps need of grand symbolic gestures by the churches to help themselves and others realise they are serious about reconciliation. One such

---

5. 'Imprisoned within Structures', Colum Kenny, ed, *The Role of Believing Communities in Building Peace in Ireland, The Believers' Enquiry*, Glencree, 1998, p 181.

6. cf. op. cit., p 186.

7. An Interchurch Group on Faith and Politics, *Breaking Down the Enmity*, 1993.

gesture, in line with John Paul II's millennial thinking, might be a common confession of guilt. More ambitious, but perhaps more relevant, would be a decisive disassociation on the Protestant side from contentious Orange marches, and on the Catholic side a more generous interpretation of the directives for eucharistic sharing. It is to this latter issue that I now turn.

3. Eucharistic sharing as symbol of reconciliation

The recent teaching document on the eucharist, *One Bread One Body*,[8] has been given a mixed reception. Broadly speaking one notes a difference between professional ecumenists and the wider general public in terms of this reception. Many professionals are conscious of the advances that the document has made, and give it a cautious welcome. The general public, on the other hand, tends to assess it unfavourably in the light of contemporary sensitivities and practice, and by contrast with the political progress that has been made. What is one to make of this difference in reception?

It is true, with the professionals, that the document represents modest progress. This can be seen, *inter alia,* in the frequent references to joint ecumenical statements, the real longing for unity that permeates the document, the appeal (as opposed to command) to Catholics to listen to its teaching, and above all the spelling out (in line with the call to Episcopal Conferences of the 1993 Directory) of occasions when exceptions may be permitted to the normal prohibition of eucharistic sharing with Protestants in a Catholic church. One welcomes this kind of progress, and it may be built on. I do note that in accordance with the same Directory the South African bishops saw the possibility of going further than our own ones in several respects.[9] So, for example, they do not restrict communion in the case of mixed marriages to a once-off event: rather they allow it to happen infrequently, and if frequently they ask that permission be sought. They refuse in general to speak of 'unique' events (the language used by *One Bread One Body*), but allow for a continuing situation where eucharistic hospitality may be allowed. Outside the mixed marriage situation they allow for eucharistic hospitality at special feasts or events. And in the case of the Catholic who wishes to receive communion in a church of the Reformation, they note, with *One Bread One Body*, the difficulty concerning the recognition of ministries, but this does not lead them to a blanket veto. Rather they content themselves with saying: 'As regards the churches arising out of the divisions that occurred in the west

8. Catholic Bishops' Conference of England & Wales, Ireland, and Scotland, *One Bread One Body*, 1998.
9. *Doctrine and Life*, 48, 1998, pp 368-378.

at the time of the Reformation, the matter, from a Catholic perspective, is not so clear.' (6.5.5) It is interesting to see the same set of Vatican directives being interpreted more liberally by a different hierarchy. I note too that, according to *The Tablet*,[10] the German bishops and the diocese of Brisbane have gone beyond the notion of 'unique' events proposed by our bishops. It remains to be seen how these different interpretations may be viewed by the Vatican itself.

Of greater interest perhaps is the question as to why the reaction of the general public has been so negative. I propose that an analysis of why this is so may be helpful in pointing us towards a theology of eucharistic sharing more in tune with the challenges of the post-Good Friday Agreement. It seems that the general public has a sense that theologians and bishops are nit-picking and being territorial, at a time when a more generous response is called for. Now, is this an example of the *sensus fidelium,* or of an uneducated and hasty trivialising and confusion of religion with politics? A discernment is required.

Suppose one accepts that the Mass is central to Catholic identity; that there is a great Protestant fear of Roman Catholicism in Northern Ireland (Home rule is Rome rule); and that therefore the excluding tendency within Roman Catholic eucharistic discipline is bound to fuel Protestant fears about the malign influence of Catholicism. In this context, it would make sense, if at all possible, to interpret the 1993 Directory generously (as the Faith and Politics group suggests in their key, basic principle). But how could one do so without compromise in the invalid sense? Well, suppose for a moment that the 'certain circumstances' in which eucharistic sharing is permitted – danger of death, but also 'grave and pressing need', including 'grave spiritual need' – could be interpreted in a wider sense than heretofore. In the document itself, it seems to me, grave and pressing need is interpreted either in an individualistic, an interpersonal, or an ecclesial way (e.g. at an ordination, the non-Catholic spouse at a mixed marriage, etc). Suppose 'need' is extended to include the socio-cultural-political context? Is not this a category extension already commonplace in official church documents (structures of sin/grace, etc)? The social is more than the interpersonal, and it is more than the ecclesial. The church is for the kingdom, for the world ... if people are so divided in Northern Ireland that they kill one another and hate one another, and if there is a religious dimension to this, then cannot this be used to extend the exceptive instances of eucharistic sharing, always supposing that the four

10. *The Tablet*, October 3rd, 1998, p 127.

conditions are in place (that the person be unable to have recourse to the eucharist from a minister of his or her own church; that they ask for the sacrament of their own initiative; that they manifest Catholic faith in the sacrament; that they be properly disposed)? Liberation theology has taught us that the social is a properly theological category; and that, as Paul understood in his eucharistic teaching in the context of rich and poor in Corinth, the secular world may be part of the critically discerned context of a theology and spirituality that refuse to be dualistic in outlook.

I appreciate the deep sensitivities that are involved in this issue of eucharistic hospitality. The desire not to compromise central truths of faith, not to confuse religion and politics in a reductionist way, is both proper and admirable. However, I have indicated the theological grounds for a more generous interpretation that is, I believe, neither compromising nor reductionist. One of the great strengths of the Roman Catholic Church is its ability to maintain unity. However, this strength, grounded in central authority and in a clear legal system, struggles to co-exist with a greater realisation of the principle of collegiality and that of the *sensus fidelium*. It is striking with regard to the latter, for example, how importantly it is taken as a theological principle in influencing the promotion of the causes of would-be blesseds and saints in the church, but how little purchase it has in other areas of church life. Similarly, it often seems that a legal approach can dominate over an approach which favours values, something which commonly happens in civil life also, but which we do well to avoid. Too often lawyers give rather than take instruction from their clients. In the Irish situation that I have described, with adequate theological and pastoral reasons in support, might it not be an authentic exercise of church leadership to say to the canonists, 'This is how we wish to proceed: find us a legal way of doing so'?

One of the professionals who is not happy with *One Bread One Body*, Enda McDonagh, articulates the same kinds of concerns: 'The belief that consultation was as usual unnecessarily limited and that canonical regulation finally took precedence over theological agreement or pastoral awareness seem borne out by the structure and content of the document itself.'[11] McDonagh interestingly sub-titles his piece 'A millennial proposal for sharing the eucharist', and goes on to say: 'For the baptised believers in Jesus Christ and in his saving, reconciling presence in the eucharist, sharing the eucharist is the crucial manifestation and means of that reconciliation. The

---

11. E. McDonagh, 'Invite and Encourage – A millennial proposal for sharing the Eucharist', *The Furrow*, 50, 1999, (18-25) p 18.

thrust of this proposal is that members of other churches with a basic belief in the eucharist as instituted by Jesus Christ should be invited and encouraged to participate in the Catholic eucharist as a manifestation and means of developing reconciliation between Christians and of witnessing to the world.'[12]

Conclusion

I have argued for a critical role for theology and religion in relation to politics; for a theology of reconciliation in post-agreement Northern Ireland; and for a more generous interpretation of eucharistic hospitality as one important instance of this kind of theology of reconciliation. It seems to me that the form of the latter argument gives grounds for hoping that one may acknowledge with the professionals the progress being made in *One Bread One Body*, and yet learn to build on this by acknowledging the extent to which popular impatience may indeed be a carrier for the stirrings of the Holy Spirit.

Much of this may seem too ambitious at a time when the Roman Catholic Church in Ireland finds itself in a distinctly weak position. The understandable temptation for leadership in particular must be to conserve, to circle the wagons and hold on to what can be salvaged. But a vision can fire the imagination and unleash energy so that, in creative fidelity to the best of the past, we may respond to the exigencies of our own time and rediscover the truth of the Pauline dictum that in our own weakness we may discover the strength of the Lord. (2 Cor 12:7-10)

---

12. McDonagh, op. cit., 20.

Politics Mirroring Society [1]

Denis Carroll

I: OUR POLITICS REFLECTS OUR SOCIETY

Ireland's political system is based upon representative democracy. In the twenty-six counties, its symbols are officially republican. 'Nationhood', 'people-hood' and 'national pride' are much spoken-of, although their content is assumed rather than examined. More recently, our political ideology approaches social democracy – although globalism and its local 'tiger' version have attacked that fragile growth. Since 1997, President McAleese's leader-ship has earned respect and affection. The Presidency enjoys deserved prestige even as other institutions are viewed with cynicism.

Living as we do in a 'globalised' context, we meet bewilderingly new issues. These affect our national ideals, trading practices and monetary policy. Within a global economy, *realpolitik* imposes the harsher 'values' of compet-itiveness and acquisition. To a degree, the dominant values of Western capital-ism bid fair to excise more generous social concern. Already, startling changes are noticeable in Irish self-perception, consumption patterns and social expectations. EU policy now affects our internal legislation ranging from equal pay to marriage laws. Entry to the NATO-led Partnership for Peace raises considerable debate. As to 'neutrality', this somewhat flaccid concept requires scrutiny in view of our nebulous foreign policy. Our political system can no longer hide behind pious platitudes or non-committal utterances if it is to play a worthwhile role on the international stage.

To avoid naïvete, one thing has to be said: our politics reflects our society. In a democracy, we get the institutions we deserve. Our political successes and failures mirror our values and aspirations. We cannot scapegoat other

---

1. A Health Warning! This chapter is prejudiced. First, it views official pronouncements with suspicion. A recent lesson is that no institution can be trusted with self-regulation or self-excul-pation. Second, it argues that theology and church should observe due humility. 'Physician, heal thyself' is appropriate here as elsewhere. Third, the author too has benefited from civil and ecclesiastical institutions. Hence, in using 'we', he realises that the word is ambiguous. To put it ungrammatically: who is 'we'?; who are 'they'? Fourth, how do 'we' know that other abuses are not hidden within 'our' institutions? Since 'we' haphazardly discovered major injustices, 'we' cannot simply draw a line on the past – 'we' must admit possible injustices today. Fifth, because the chapter is an exercise in social theology, it seeks positive elements which might help in the future.

times and other people for shortcomings in our own attitudes. If ever it was such, post-modern Ireland is no longer the island of saints and scholars. As a society it is decent but conservative. In a precarious balance, compassion meets callousness, co-operation turns into competition. A desire for honesty co-exists with hypocrisy on uncomfortable issues. At a time of unprecedented national prosperity – with a £5bn budgetary surplus in 1999 – we evade radical measures to address deprivation and exclusion. Amongst the electorate, vigorous policies on inclusion and justice are not always welcome. Hence, they are rarely attempted. Whereas once – even in the 1980s – emigration was a major problem, now, sadly, immigration is perceived to be a threat.

Issues undreamt-of in previous generations have changed our political landscape. The interpretation of 'Sinn Féin' as communitarian self-reliance is overtaken by a selfishness more aptly described as 'Mé Féin' (myself alone). If, to date, we have escaped the worst *fin-de-siècle* excesses, this may be due to residual ideals and a modicum of decency in the society. Yet, can we presume that the ideals will endure? Do we overestimate the 'modicum of decency'?

Certainly, disillusion is palpable. It becomes increasingly difficult to speak of a national project or shared ideals. In regard to once cherished institutions, trust is now at a minimum. It is the age of hidden agendas and 'spin doctors'. Politicians, judiciary and clergy have been found wanting. Double standards, cruelty to children in institutional care, unfairness in administration of the law, 'golden circles' in business and politics, have been starkly documented. Disturbing questions remain. Did we half-knowingly tolerate scandals uncovered in so many of our institutions? And if 'we' did not know, how can 'we' say things are now different? Did we encourage church and state to maintain 'a class-ridden, at times tyrannical social structure'? Did a false consensus inflict a series of injustices? Did a concept of God as moral-policeman ensure that those at the bottom of the social hierarchy were neglected, discounted and mistreated?

These questions do not overlook the fact that, in great majority, clergy, politicians and professionals work honourably to the ethics of their calling. They share the commitment to fair play which marks so many Irish people. Yet, we have to avoid self-congratulation or complacency. If this essay argues against cynicism it does not condone a sorry catalogue. Scandals *have* abounded – political, financial, medical, judicial and clerical. They were uncovered not by institutions themselves but by accident or as victims broke the silence. Official talk about 'self-correcting mechanisms', 'checks and balances', etc., remains unconvincing. It is important to investigate how an ideal was tarnished. Did we all assist in the process either through laziness or self-interest? How far are we prepared to work for genuine social inclusion and justice for all? Recently, Fr Brendan Devlin argued that the question no longer is 'who are we as Irish people?' but rather 'what do we wish to become?'. In other words, the future raises moral questions as well as economic ones.[2]

Do we suffer amnesia on the best of our ideals? Do we run away from genuinely radical challenges? To seek a self-critical principle does not ignore the need for realism. Nor does it pretend that principles can be reduced to trite formulae. However, we need a yardstick to measure our performance, to recognise what is unacceptable, to have some ideal for which to work. Platitudes about 'democratic institutions', etc. are unsatisfactory. Like socialist or liberal rhetoric, they are debased currency. Moving into a new millennium we have to decide what to bring from our past. As a society, can we recover a self-critical principle to measure our ideals and self-deceptions? Is there a principle which, like Exodus 22, implants a subversive memory to monitor our performance and indicate a way forward: 'Do not ill-treat or oppress a stranger. Remember that you were strangers in Egypt.' (Exodus 22:21)?

II: LESSONS FROM THE PAST – AN AMBIGUOUS PERFORMANCE

Since 1922, the Irish state espoused a social project, based on highly charged symbols. 'Cherishing all the children of the nation', 'equality before the law', 'indefeasible rights of citizens' – all these were the coinage of official discourse. Ideals of republican morality articulated in the years 1916-22 were frequently cited. Stemming from resistance to colonial oppression, they embodied an alternative project for 'the Irish people'. Admitting the diversity of Irish society and recognising our global responsibilities, what do we make of these expressions? Do they have real content? Are we somehow ashamed of them?

Pragmatism and realism are dominant concepts as Ireland fights for its place among the 'developed countries'. Such 'realism' threatens to diminish solidarity with the poor or the excluded. We are not exempt from Noam Chomsky's prediction that the poor and the immigrant will be seen as the enemies of continued success. Where success is equated with virtue it is but a short step to saying that 'losers' are culpable – a new version of *vae victis* (away with the conquered). Decent traditional values are then replaced by

---

2. Brendan Devlin, 'Seastán na Gaeilge i margadh mór na cruinne', *Irish Times,* July 14, 1999. This fine article examines the place of Irish in a globalised market.

tawdry self-advertisement. In regard to recent performance, there is little cause for complacency. Behind newly found wealth, Ireland still has pockets of deprivation and exclusion. Unequal access to health care and serious housing problems remind us that many are excluded in the midst of plenty. Inequality of opportunity is far from a thing of the past. One commentator put it: 'As we look at the administration of justice, the operations of banks, the links between business and politics – it is plain that the most pervasive influence on Irish society is class. Class governs access to health services, housing and education; the work we do, the environment we live in, the air we breathe.'[3] Can we tolerate such exclusion complacently?

Hence, we should be modest in claiming that earlier, more radical ideals have been attained. These did exist but are not integrated into our political system. They were represented by people like Michael Davitt, James Connolly and Peadar O'Donnell. Davitt's views on land reform went beyond 'peasant proprietorship' – it included agricultural and industrial workers. Connolly debunked the assumption that political independence would automatically bring social justice. The 1913 lock-out showed that nationalist ideology did not exclude harshness to urban workers. As a result, Connolly insisted that native greed was as virulent as foreign rapacity. O'Donnell discerned an innate conservatism at the core of Irish nationalism. It is worth noting that Davitt, Connolly and O'Donnell met ill-concealed hostility from church, state and many Irish people. For decades, strong farmers and businessmen were cosseted, while urban and agricultural labourers were virtually ignored. After independence, Ireland was not a happy place for unmarried mothers, the urban poor and, as we increasingly learn, for children in the 'care' of state institutions.

Do some count for more than others?
It can be argued that the shortfall was due to human frailty. Likewise, it can be said that Ireland was no worse than – and in some instances better than – other societies. This, however, will not do. It can be a facile alibi, a denial of festering problems. Critical examination discloses that today's problems gestated for longer than we care to admit. From mid-nineteenth century, Ireland was conservative in religion and politics. Long before independence, class consciousness and social control were the common link of Maynooth and Dublin Castle. Obsession with 'property rights' had little sympathy with radical politics urged by Davitt, Connolly and O'Donnell. In broad terms, the

3. Dick Walsh, 'A Shameful Silence As The Children Suffered', *Irish Times,* 1 May, 1999.

people of no property ranked at the bottom of the social hierarchy (if they ranked at all). Class consciousness rigidly divided the labourer from the tenant farmer, the poor from the 'respectable'. For all too long, poverty was criminalised, e.g vagrants and children living in poverty. Quite clearly, some people did count for more than others.

A 'stake in the country' mentality was implicit even in the independence movement. The first Dáil (1919-1920) was nervous about land redistribution. After a tragic civil war (1922-23), the new state did undertake modest reconstruction. Rural electrification, water schemes, some reforms in education, social housing programmes, promotion of Irish language and culture, were a partial fulfillment of the first Dáil's programme (January 1919). Yet, beneath the surface, multiple exclusions prevailed. The unemployed or politically dissident were feared and sometimes forced to emigrate. Land reform and economic redistribution were kept under tight rein. This was not due to 'foreign' influence but rather to pressure from sectional interests. Social criticism was deemed a Communist threat. Paranoia about subversion (a 'Red scare' in the early 1930s) made it a difficult time for alternative political thought. Major beneficiaries were the professionals, the middle classes and strong farmers whose interests were jealously preserved. Although liberal orthodoxy now blames the Catholic Church, Peadar O'Donnell's acerbic remark is true – it was not that Irish society was priest-ridden but rather that it was driven by middle class, economically conservative interests. A two-tiered society lay beneath the official ideology of 'peoplehood'.

From 1932, despite some improvements, a new government by Fianna Fáil ('The Republican Party') was unable to fashion an inclusive society. It did release political prisoners, institute slum clearance and help small farmers. Nevertheless, the real forces in the socio-political process were not disturbed. Access to education, medical services and economic advancement eluded both urban and rural poor. At the Sinn Féin Ard Fheis (1935), Fr Michael O'Flanagan's radical voice expressed a sense of disillusion. According to O'Flanagan, 'officialdom' had not changed since colonial days. The official mind remained 'the real master of Ireland'. Meanwhile, post-colonial attitudes and a complacent 'morality' penalised all who did not 'measure up'. While state institutions were nominally fair, the interests of landed or industrial property were paramount in practical politics and administration of the law. For all its merits, the 1937 Constitution lent support to those who resisted economic reform. The principle of 'private property' overrode the 'common good'. Even in the late 1960s, the Kenny report (to facilitate land acquisition for social housing) was stymied by propertied interests.

Theological quiescence?

Was there an unspoken collaboration of church and state? With rare but remarkable exceptions, churchmen did not criticise the state.[4] For a while, Ireland aimed to become 'the greatest Catholic country in the world'. It suited the prosperous to display their religious loyalties. Altogether, it was a bad bargain for social criticism. A conservative church made clear its opposition to a welfare state. In such circumstances, a 'respectable' church did not challenge the state on widespread poverty and rampant emigration. Courageous statements from Bishop Duigenan (Clonfert) and Archbishop McQuaid's social initiatives were honourable exceptions. Nevertheless, critical social analysis as we speak of it today hardly existed. It was as if a pragmatic bargain had been struck: the state did not trespass on ecclesiastical interests; the church limited its public concern to narrowly defined 'moral' questions.

Yet, real achievements were attained which it would be unfair to overlook. National and local politics retained a basic ethic of public service. Despite shortcomings of 'the official mind', the latter maintained a careful integrity. As Joe Lee has shown, there were residual decencies in Irish politics. If these did not attain full potential it was due to innate caution which favoured the *status quo*. Sincere attempts were made to include the different churches in the new society. Nor can clerical failings obliterate good work done by church people for and with the poor. Some innovations planted lasting seeds, mainly in the community sector. For example, Fr John Hayes's Muintir na Tíre worked for a sustainable local economy. At a time of increased centralisation, priests and bishops spoke of 'community'. Fr Hayes insisted on democracy at parish level. So did Fr Devane SJ and Fr Gaynor in Clare. Many years later, Fr James McDyer introduced thinking which predated liberation theology. Remarkably, McDyer brought his practical vision to communities throughout the land. According to his autobiographical memoir, he received, at best, a mixed reception in official circles. It would be ungenerous to overlook the pioneering work of a Fr Tom Fehily or a Victor Bewley in their courageous work for travellers.

'Modernisation'

With a considerable jump, one turns to the 'modernisation' of Irish society. The key date is 1959 when Sean Lemass and T. K. Whitaker launched a new

---

4. Facile anti-clericalism is unjust to many clergy who spoke for justice often at cost to themselves. Some present day voices are mentioned in this essay – they include sisters, brothers and priests. Gerald Moran's *Radical Irish Priests* details the contribution of several forgotten clerical voices. There are many more.

programme for economic expansion. Central to the programme were economic development and adaptation to free trade. Emphasis shifted to projects defined in economist terms. With the claim that 'a rising tide raises all boats', the politics of production overrode the politics of redistribution. Yet, since the politics of production were skewed in the direction of the already prosperous, the poor remained for many years in the mud flats of poverty and unemployment. In the early days of economic programmes the chief beneficiaries were professionals, officials and developers. Much of the physical heritage was destroyed in a frenzy of demolition for industrial 'development'. A 'get rich quick' mentality was reinforced – a forerunner of the 'payments to politicians' difficulties which today cost so much to the public purse. Despite much talk of development, insufficient attention was given to the question of *appropriate* development. Whatever development took place by-passed marginal communities in inner cities and the west of Ireland.

Other influences changed the face of Ireland. The post-1969 'troubles' brought loss of life and widespread suffering. Repressive legislation induced a culture of official secrecy and duplicity. The policy of 'seeing no evil or hearing no evil' about treatment of the minority community in Northern Ireland reaped a miserable reward. It took many years before official politics admitted the reality of such injustice and discrimination. Entry to the then EEC brought reappraisal of illiberal laws, on the positive side, and loss of the better values of 'peoplehood', on the negative. Although cohesion funds from Brussels enabled infrastructural improvements and economic expansion, our political thinking was marked by narrow self-interest to the neglect of more generous instincts.

The 'global village' has brought disruption as well as wealth. There have been improvements in unemployment figures and cessation of forced emigration. Yet, drug abuse and alienation among young people should prevent self-congratulation. Extreme individualism now drives out solidarity and compassion. Egregious wealth mocks grinding poverty. A comfortable 'middle class' looks to property values and practises a frequently ridiculous 'gentrification'. Travellers still experience discrimination. Refugees are treated with niggardly suspicion. *Realpolitik* excuses selfishness and ruthlessness. Calls for inclusion and social justice are dismissed as 'begrudgery' and 'anti-enterprise'. Nevertheless, a difficult question remains to be faced. Is the emergent selfishness traceable only to these new pressures? Is our political ethic implicitly selfish? Are our inherited values able to insist on the Judaeo-Christian demand for justice to the excluded?

III: COUNTERVOICES?

In a recent study, Desmond Fennell remarks on the weakness of social analysis in nineteenth-century Irish Christianity. The radical voices did not come from the churches but rather from James Bronterre O'Brien, Feargus O'Connor, James Fintan Lalor and, later, Michael Davitt. It is not suggested that the churches were supine. In October 1847, the Irish bishops protested to Lord Lieutenant Clarendon that the primary right to life was sacrificed to 'the incessant reclamations of the *subordinate* rights of property'. (This ordering of rights should be noted.) Frs Thomas O'Shea and Matthew O' Keefe, (the Callan Curates), Fr James O'Dwyer (Limerick) and countless other clergy worked for famine victims. They raised critical voices and pioneered a movement for land reform (Frs O'Shea and O'Keeffe). Yet, they had to contend with official suspicion and the control instincts of Cardinal Cullen. Brendan Ó Cathaoir's fine book, *Famine Diary*, presents the unforgettable analysis of Bishop Thomas Lynch (Toronto) – but even Dr Lynch had to emphasise that no 'subversion' was intended. Again, Gerald Moran's *Radical Irish Priests* documents imaginative analysis of by now forgotten clerical voices. It would be unjust to overlook the labours of other Christian groups, e.g. the Society of Friends ('Quakers') and clergy of the Protestant churches, some of whom gave their lives in ministering to famine stricken people.

Yet it has to be said that in theology the dominant pattern was otherwise. There was little analysis of political/social mechanisms. Only in the 1970s – after Vatican II and the first Synod of bishops – did social justice as a 'constitutive element' of preaching the gospel come to the fore. Another valuable principle was accentuated, viz. those who preach justice have themselves to practice that virtue. In Ireland, various commissions raised justice issues. Pre-eminent were the Justice and Peace Commission, Trócaire and the bishops' Council for Social Welfare. In the Church of Ireland, several valuable documents on social responsibility were published. The Catholic bishops' pastoral, *The Work of Justice* (1977), applied social justice principles more concretely than heretofore. Reflecting Paul VI's emphasis, the bishops moved from the 'rights' of private property to the duties attaching to wealth. They criticised selfish disregard for the rights of the poor. To a degree, the bishops' pastoral was ineffective since its principles did not enter the mainstream of Irish social thinking. The emphasis on justice lacked the energy of places like Latin America where national hierarchies devoted consistent attention to social transformation.

Meanwhile, the religious – priests, brothers and nuns – 'voted with their feet'. That is to say, they lived in marginalised areas and raised poverty issues. Diocesan clergy were frequently the first 'professionals' into new suburbs in Dublin, Cork, Waterford, Galway and Limerick. With skill and dedication, Sister Stanislaus Kennedy brought homelessness to the forefront. Jesuit priests set up communities in Ballyfermot, Ballymun and Portadown. Fr Peter McVerry became a central figure in the care of homeless youths. The Jesuit Centre for Faith and Justice published valuable works of social analysis. A group of Jesuits published a timely book on 'social solidarity'. In many places, there was a reversal whereby returned missionaries applied insights learned in South America and elsewhere to the 'home' situation. The focus of this essay permits all too brief reference to the work of the late Fr Michael Sweetman, SJ and Fr Austin Flannery, OP. Likewise, the prophetic stances of Fr Desmond Wilson must be saluted.

Perhaps the most sustained analysis has come from CORI's justice desk. Countless publications by Fr Sean Healy and Sister Bridget Reynolds affected socio-political discourse in Ireland. Inclusiveness, partnership, human rights and environmental responsibility, budgetary policy, poverty and 'minimum income' have been skillfully addressed with up-to-date analysis. As a result, CORI's voice gains increasing credence among policy makers at local and national levels. In May 1999, CORI's *Social Partnership In A New Century* indicates a way forward for Irish society facing the millennium. This publication runs a wide gamut with its emphasis on right relationships with self, God, family, institutions and the global environment. Helpfully, it reiterates the interconnection of rights and duties for such relationships. Its citation of Hans Küng's proposals for a global ethic is relevant to the Irish context: 'the right to a secure life, equitable treatment, an opportunity to earn a fair living, the definition and preservation of peoples' differences through peaceful means, participation in governance at all levels, free and fair petition for redress of gross injustices, equal access to information and to the global commons.' (*Social Partnership in a New Century,* pp 59-60)

IV: RECOVERY OF A PROPHETIC VOICE

As of 1999 there are many challenges to our political process. Reform of local government is proposed at a time when it is seen as weak and fragmented. In any such reform, integrity and greater democratic participation will be central. Again, in regard to national government, the same values are necessary if cynicism with the democratic system is to be halted. At time of writing, many people express worry about the lack of answerable government.

To speak of 'prophetic voice' is not to confuse religion with politics. It is simply to say that for the new millennium such a voice is more necessary than ever. In a fragmenting society where acquisitiveness predominates, respect for the poor, the sick and the aged receives less attention. Although the churches must say 'we have been unprofitable servants', they retain sufficient energy for witness to solidarity with the poor and excluded. In sacramental and institutional ways they can provide space where countervoices are heard. Their daunting task is to merit a hearing where myriad voices claim attention and where, as at present, the stock of institutional Christianity is not high.

In the 1950s, Teilhard de Chardin spoke of globalisation to explain the emergence of humankind within an evolving world. Now, globalism is a dominant socio-political concept. For good or ill, it prevails in economics, politics and the arts. It is a *zeitgeist* of which theology must take account. Yet 1990s 'globalisation' is much more complex than Chardin may have suspected. It can be defined as the increased interdependence of states, politically and economically. It is about the communications revolution and worldwide consumer patterns.[5] The 'global village' may be an exhilarating place for the young, the computer literate and the wealthy. It is a hard place for the excluded – the old, the unlettered and the poor. It is more unequal than ever – 20% of people account for 80% of global consumption. Here, the oft-quoted saying is true: the rich get richer while the poor get poorer. Global trade has expanded but mainly at the expense of the poor.

What, then, is the world of which 'we' are citizens? Here again, the interests of dominant groups seem to define 'world'. Suffering in one part of the world counts for less than in Europe or North America. Although there is cheap talk about morality and solidarity, the varied reactions to the phenomenon of suffering displays self-interest on the part of the strong. *Realpolitik* dictated a shameful silence on East Timor both in Europe and Australia. Would the Gulf War have occurred were it not to safeguard powerful economic interests? What interests were at work in the Balkans war of 1999?

We cannot predict the future. Yet, we can extrapolate from present problems. If 'we' are citizens of one world, who counts as 'we'? In the new world order are all people respected for their human dignity? Is it simply those who are white or wealthy or citizens of powerful states? In an Ireland predicated on republican democracy, is our use of 'we' unreal and exclusive? Is there 'par-

---

5. This working definition of 'globalisation' is given in Denis Carroll, *Land*, Trócaire-Veritas-Cafod, Dublin and London, 1998, p 13.

ity of esteem' in any real sense? What of travellers? What of refugees? What of the poor in urban ghettoes? What of the rural poor? Does not 'we' ring hollow when inequality of access to employment, education, housing and health services can still be documented. In an Ireland where the league of super-rich, rich and also-rans makes its appearance, is 'we' more than a convenient fiction, a mask for real injustices? Does the Celtic Tiger bite some people even as it brings undreamt prosperity to others? When prevailing economic forces laud selfish individualism, then critical reflection on 'we' language becomes more necessary than ever.

In economic terms, reality is defined by profitability. A further step is to glorify efficiency at the cost of humanity. Financial gain and pragmatism become the total range of aspiration. A genuinely Christian voice will declare that success is not everything, that we 'do not live by bread alone'. In concrete terms, this means critique of dominant utilitarian values. Mobile investment, so much vaunted in recent years, is exactly what its says. It devastates one set of livelihoods as it moves for greater profit to a 'cheaper' environment. Tom Hyland, an Irish human rights activist, observes that globalism is a reality when it comes to business but not in regard to human rights.

Short of a worldwide cataclysm, the new era cannot be reversed. To ignore it would be self-defeating, akin to nostalgia for medieval times. Rather, the possibilities within the new millennium should be recognised and developed. Irish Christianity has many resources to face the millennium. Despite historical shortcomings, its considerable resources can be pitted to stressing the unique value of every person. A new emphasis on our responsibility for God's creation can be implemented in liturgy, catechesis and theology. In national and international context, we have powerful symbols which express universal solidarity. Our theological resources contain material for prophetic critique of exclusion and inhumaneness. The question is: have we the courage to articulate the demands of social inclusion and justice for all?

Stationing the Cross:
The minutes of a millennium

Aidan Mathews

The millennium itself is largely a matter of voodoo and numerology. The transition from BC to AD in any individual life involves endeavours of ordinance beyond the stick columns of simple arithmetic, involves in fact much travel, much travail: preparation and reparation. Besides there's a territorial triumphalism about the whole event which scarcely cares to discern in any shape or form the worst century since chronological records began.

But I'm a married man, a father of children, one who lives with his two daughters and wife in the temporary shelter of home and work, bookshelf and motor car; and I want to mark the moment in this little exfoliation of four lives, the fading and the flourishing together, because, in my middle-aged statelessness as an interim presence between geriatric infants and child-like elders, I can link my patriarchal grandparents from the Parnellite years, with their bonfires and their Roman candles at Hallowe'en, to their great grandchildren's astounded street party under a comet called Hale Bopp in the end times of two summers ago when we were all of us briefly shepherds of the asphalt junction and Magi of the filter-lights at the ring-road.

But where can I speak of such things, and in what acoustic other than that of a chapel? My married state and my medical records disbar me from its sanctuary, where the quiet dismantlement of the altar rails in my early adolescence was a seismic shudder that gave the fall of the Berlin Wall ten years ago an aura of déjà vu. My presence in the nave too is an unpredictable one, and my children's insistence on hogging the front pew in order to watch the guitars and tambourines of the folk group sits edgily with my private instinct to be back down at the west door where my own authentic people stand in their short-sleeved silhouettes with a view behind them of buses passing along the Via Sacra of the southbound carriageway. The confessionals as well, the hidey holes of Nilfisk hoovers nowadays, I have shunned for a quarter of a century, finding counsel and clarity in the ministrations of friends and the mahogany tables of psychiatrists. Only the terraces of tiny candles bring me immediate healing but the votive trolleys are not the monopoly of any tradition, Orthodox or Taoist. So it is to the stations of the cross, then, away from the ambo and the silly side altars, that I turn for a template, wanting the dignified kitsch of a few of them to divulge some small importance for the century my daughters will almost certainly see through, with their snot-nosed grandchildren misting the mantelpiece memories of a strange man with a hairline fracture in his head and a mouth that might be shouting or smiling.

Jesus is condemned to death

I am immediately at the ambiguous heart of the world I inhabit and propagate, the great Graeco-Roman law-court which stretches across the semi-detached dormitory suburbs of the Northworld from Trieste to Toronto and from Bucharest to Belfast. For the very first station in the passion pageant is no reflective encounter between equals in the mystery of a meeting but a confrontation between dais and dock: the condemned man stands and falls before the criminal justice system which annihilates him at a word, because the criminal justice system is the accredited domain of public vengeance, of exemplary retribution, and of the neo-liberal *ponziopilatismo* to which the dithering procurator lent his name. The whole Judeo-Christian discourse of forgiveness and reconciliation, of privilege and protectiveness – ransoming the vulnerable, rescuing the powerless – amounts here only to decor that distracts us from the brutalising empiricism of law and order in an Enlightenment realm; and that continuing economy – Satanic at least in the literal sense, since Satan is the Syriac term for a legal prosecutor – tolerates the confession and the sign of peace in our Sunday eucharist as the pastel complement of its own tablets of stone. We exchange pardon in a state full of prisons.

Pilate and Jesus. It is not a distant spectacle but a proximate terror. It is a terror because Justice, the Latin for getting even, still has the last word in every Christian state and safeguards my apologetic shelves. It is a terror because intrepid suburbanites like myself, the shepherds by night of Neighbourhood Watch, have limited faith to the regulated centre of life and not centred it instead at the irregularity of its serrating limits where violence and violation thrive; so governance and goodwill, a kind of homogenised Galilean dailiness of let-be and love-each-other, has neutered the tremendous summons to the rubbish dump as the fractured ground of God. And it is a terror because in our haste since the mid-nineteenth century to accomplish a Roman Catholic citadel, we had forgotten first principles: that the Christ is always beyond the encampment, beyond domesticity, in the place of exclusion, in the place of oppression, the place of spittle and saliva, of loathing and prurience; and he is there as a condemned criminal, suspended between two other condemned criminals who are hardly aware, either of them, that they occupy the very assignments at his right and his left hand side which Jesus denied to James and John, the vertical sectarians.

Irish writers have traditionally championed the liminal individual, the ejected and dejected one. In this they have the escort of scripture for it is the

Hebrew Bible and the Christian New Testament, rather than the storylines of classical myth, which represent the outcast as the alias of the Most High and the alibi of the Lord. But it takes a true semite to recognise the lamb of God in the black sheep and the scapegoat in the culprit, and I am mostly gentile. The binary mindset of my waking state deals always and everywhere, naturally and normally, in right and wrong, in good and bad, in the dualist mandate. Popular culture and the popular media may do the same in their hypnotic symmetries of victimised and victimiser, and even literature invests densely in caricatural figures as the sinister foils of truly heroic characters. Tragedy itself, the aristocratic form *par excellence,* began as *trag odos* (the root of the goat), the stoned procession of the levitical goat. So the culture of disclosure which we find both in European and American broadsheets and tabloids perhaps draws some of its strength from an accusatory primal narrative in which we all share. These legends of the id, whether in censorious editorials or in forensic reportage, reveal thereby our own gluttonous habituation to the tales of guilt and innocence in their theatrical dialectics of indictment and acquittal, and it may be that we cannot expel such sagas altogether because expulsion is their *raison d'être.*

When I was a child, the culture I grew up in taught me to beware of the homosexual man and to be wary of the Protestant clergyman; thirty years later my children learn from bulletins, billboards and the condensing Zeitgeist to beware of Catholic priests and male heterosexuals. The scapegoats change but the slingstones don't. So we get even and we get odder. Yet the deep befriending of the victim, which is the prime biblical bond, can be a falsified value if it only demonises the victimiser and sentimentalises the innocent. Then the casualties become angels and the defendants monsters in a process in which it is sometime hard to separate prosecution from persecution and in which everyone's humanity is commodified. Throughout the temperate zone both print and electronic media select and deselect the strangers we are to despise, and prejudice mutates within us with the inventiveness of a virus. But our everlasting need to narrate our journeys as a sum of personal vindications against the vileness of others is countered by the corrective tartness in the first of the stations of the cross which demands, instead, our advocacy of the worst sorts in an adversarial world: the *status quo* and the filthy convict remain forever a stumbling block that refuses to be chiselled into an edifying cornerstone.

When am I going to learn that the people who bear the wounds of Christ are not the haloed celibates with runny palms in the discount mysticism of consumer religiosity? The people who carry the stigmata are the people I stigmatise. And when am I going to learn that the love of neighbour has at the heart of its homeliness the dreadful injunction to love my enemy?

Jesus is loaded with the Cross

In an act of identification with the categories of criminality which disgust us, Jesus is himself heavy laden. Now some of our crosses are visible. Some achieve high prestige. Some are almost deemed to be evidence of election. Multiple sclerosis in this sense gets a better press than manic depression; the loss of a child outweighs the death of an adult. There are classes of loss and of endurance which are universally admitted and admired, a taxonomy of wounds. This is perhaps as it ought to be. But there are also crosses which are deemed to be double-crosses, more compromised than promising, more sufferance than suffering, and these include the choices and circumstances of many of my friends who are rarely if ever invited to the demure forums of anthologies which seek to paperback the depths.

I ate recently with some companions who share with me a rich, even a replete, origin in the Roman Catholic culture – often more a matter of Catholicism than of catholicity – that Ireland in the 60s and 70s embodied, but whom their own ethical instincts have forced to the periphery – some would say the horizon – of the practice of faith. It isn't perhaps so much that they are either non-Christian or post-Christian in the very challenging ways in which those prophetic presences endow us now more than ever, but that neither temple nor synagogue, cult or classroom, answer adequately the call of their complex lives. Besides, in their heterosexuality and in their homosexuality, in their separate mysteries and in their separated relationships, in the most interior places of their human endeavour, in their very sanctuary, in fact, they feel unworthy – rather like the woman who wept beside me at a wedding once because her marriage feast at Cana had turned in due course and in due process into the Canon Law on marriage, and her table fellowship into a tribunal; and she felt unclean. Basically, none of us at the table could share food at the altar.

The body of Christ is a versatile organism. Many ordinary Christians, both lay and religious, are hospitable to persons who've been marginalised by their own charisms or by their own case-histories. But acts of discreet eucharistic generosity or the gestures of outreach by individual parishioners to women and men whose relational holiness is still illegal and cannot officially be celebrated as the venue of Yahweh, do not compensate, in the command economy of a terraced church, for the non-negotiable displeasure of the managerial tier, which percolates and pervades the works. I am not speaking here of Christ incarnate. I am speaking of Christianity Incorporated. The truth is, that the way and the life are more important than the solemnised tones of systematic theology, just as finally and fundamentally the Beatitudes matter more than the Creed. There have never been so many god-fearers in the Courtyard of the Gentiles, and they are withheld from stepping over the threshold not by fear of circumcision but by the personal mutilations which ecclesiastical protocol and propriety insist upon. If we do not restore the dual mandate of Peter and Paul, if we do not mess with the gentiles in their glittering cities instead of cowering behind our word-processed newsletters, we will become another version of rabbinic Judaism, pure and protectionist, rather than the comrades of a burly, vernacular walk-about which we call primitive Christianity on pilgrimage.

When am I going to learn that the way is the wayside, and that Pentecost is the opposite of Babel? When am I going to learn that I am not building a tower to reach to heaven but a dance-floor for the horizontal planet and that the gift of tongues has nothing to do with dumbstruck rabbitings and every-thing to do with speaking to the other in her own language?

Jesus falls three times
It's August now, the month we regard as autumn and the English as summer, the honorific month of Caesar Augustus who, as patron of the census which sought to name and number every detail of the whole inhabited world, is surely the patron saint of positivism and the supreme secularist. As the results of the school-leavers' state examinations are published, the sight of the cult-ure of certification which accompanies every Irish person from uterus to hearse would surely please the calculating *pontifex maximus* of imperial Rome: the linearity of a *curriculum vitae,* with its clockwork increments of application and dividend, is much more Roman than Palestinian; and the near Eastern fables which speak to us of a wave-form, of a paschal arc, in the momentum of every life at sea, and the age-old Jewish profession that failure and fall, trespass and reversal, are the modalities of the soul on shank's mare, cannot be heard above the propaganda which trumpets the higher human content of a time-tabled photo-fit professional lifestyle in the white-collar continent.

So Jesus falls, and falls again: not once or twice but a third time too, in the threefold sacral stumbling which thereby authorises our attention and our imitation. What is most unearthly in the Christ of God is precisely his earthenness; and the gravitational lapses of the three devotional panels which portray his proneness to fall flat repeat the incarnational trajectory of the Word made flesh. We must therefore cherish imperfection or go mad in the very middle of our lives where we are always and everywhere shambles and chancel at one and the same time.

None of this is new, obviously, but much of it has been retired from the lectern. Most of my post-Christian friends who sit respectfully through church services at the great mission opportunities of the millennium – bap-tisms, weddings and funerals – do not identify themselves as Catholics or communicants, because their spirituality is more adult than the (per)version of religion they have discarded or because they are conscientious as well as conscientised and believe that they cannot, in good faith, present either their goodness or their faith as a sufficiency, without damaging both. Their pain has not been lived or liturgised. For if the loutishness of clerical power in the years of my birth and background antagonised one part of the population into an anecdotal and unexamined anti-clericalism, it was the lunacy of infantile pietism which discouraged those who had suffered the complex world to come too close to them and needed now, after the crisis and the chrysalis, to be tasked with an adequate grandeur.

When am I going to learn that the gospels are written in Greek and not in Aramaic, that they have already gone beyond themselves in order to arrive at themselves? When am I going to learn that the eucharist is made for men and women and not men and women for the eucharist?

Jesus meets many women –
his mother, Veronica, and the daughters of Jerusalem
In the midst of the male gauntlet the condemned criminal is met by a female honour guard. Within the devotional tradition, as well as within the scriptural canon, women embody from the beginning the pastoral and prophetic gifts which continue today to characterise their overwhelming majority in the statistics of consecrated life. Denial of power has matured their moral authority over the centuries to the point where the eros of the first prehensile state is seen to contradict the lovingkindness of the second, and their historic asymmetry to the circles of power and privilege since the start of the church has made them the flesh and blood of the Holy Spirit in her speechless descendings.

But the meeting with Mary is not only pathetic in the sense of the loyal, lamenting presence; it is problematical too. Each of us must encounter our parents at a place that is not of our choosing; and at the terrible, disclosing close of a godawful era, we must all invigilate that appointment with the parental, the paternal, the patriarchal word, which first fashioned and then relinquished us in the apocalypse of adulthood. The funeral games of traditional Catholic nationalism began with the Papal Mass in the Phoenix Park, and continued through the scarcity and defeat of the nineteen eighties into the commemorative vigil years of a decoy Famine that actually waked the traumas of contemporary displacement; and the paedophile trials themselves crystallised the oedipal impulse in a polity which fled in consternation before all our fathers.

For those of my age and stage in life, adrift on the landing between geriatric diapers and a toddler's nappies, the nearing hiatus of the Western calendar is a suggestible rupture, a fault-line splitting charges and their chaperones, the advent of a sombre and unaccompanied journey. So the leave-taking at that last encounter with the parent, in all its desire and disappointment, must be done well. Our sanity depends upon it. For the benediction must be given, the blessing must be spoken. Otherwise, we are neither wise nor other. And perhaps the eventual understanding that our fathers were not God must include for a time the more unfortunate suspicion that God is not a father. James Simmons' great line – 'I am not Jesus Christ and neither was he' – is better theology than its poet might have intended. It provides a decent enough mantra or antiphon for the service of January.

What I mean is this. If we do not sing at night to our wheat and our tares, if we do not acknowledge the pathology in our closest relationships, if we do not affirm the dysfunction at the heart of all that is best in our family life and friendships, if, in short, we do not admit the ministry of irony and paradox and provocation into our mission, we will make a poor thing, a plaster saint, a petit bourgeois mannikin out of the image and likeness of God. We will construct an idol of banality which Jesus the Jew was a fool to die for. And it is Veronica, it seems to me, who shows the way here. After all, the three persons of God are as many masks, as many mouthpieces, for a spirit which can only be seen in the momentary, momentous mould of its passing. Yet Veronica has chosen wisely: at the moment she presses her veil to the face of the condemned man, the veil of the Temple parts to reveal for all time the face that God turns towards us. It is the face of each and every person we reject. It is the face that inspires most disgust in us. It is the face that is effaced with an anorak at the door of the courthouse. It is the blurred face of the suspect in the video rewind. As bloody and bloated as a newborn baby's, as pulverised as a boy's head in a punishment beating, it is the unlikely image and the unimaginable likeness of man.

So the pretty myth of feminine intervention hosts a modest truth. Veronica, who transforms the vicious circle of violence into the hermeneutic circle of accurate decipherment and who recognises the Lord in the way that the dog Argos recognises Odysseus on his return to Ithaca, intimately and instinctively, reminds us of how best we can conceptualise the God of our semantics: by somatising God's word in the speech acts of our life, by grounding the mystical body in the material one, by opposing our honourable nakedness to the vested resentment of the world.

I must of course come clean. Raised by a child from a convent orphanage and married to the adoptive daughter of elderly parents, I have a heightened, a heraldic sense of women's dogged magnanimity in difficult times – not only the orphaned but the surrogate mothers. My own two daughters sway unsteadily on their high shoes beside me, and it grates that their talents for patience and laughter cannot preside at the banquet. Both can wash the feet, and do; but neither can break the bread. They may go on to grow new human life with their own body and blood, to squeeze it into the world in the breaking of tissue and the pouring of liquid, to nourish it inside and outside with the sweet largesse of our gifted flesh, and still their chromosomes scandalise the holy table, served as it is by one half of our species just as the eucharist itself is served by one half of the plenary sign.

A woman gave me faith; a woman restored it to me. When am I going to learn that a human being is ordained by the things she ponders deeply in her heart and not by the angle-poise over the manuals in the bachelor's dormitory?

Simon of Cyrene helps Jesus to carry his Cross

Because I'm not a scripture scholar I'm allowed the licence to imagine this particular plaque on the wall not as an icon of timid assistance, of a yellow-pack Samaritan coerced into kindness by a Latin conscript, but as an interfaith moment of difficult mutuality. The Dispersion Jew who has left his hellenised commune to undertake a pilgrimage to the Temple is, I imagine, one who recites his Torah Talmud in the Greek Septuagint of a synagogue which, if not assimilated, has at least achieved an accommodation of a socio-cultural kind with the beautifully erotic and neurotic civilisation of the maritime powers in the Mediterranean. So he stands for all those whom we would perhaps prefer to remain sitting, for the shoreliners who are curious but not committed, distant but not detached. The work of the cross is carried forward not only by the contributions of those who are its ideological militia, but by the corporal worship and witness of the entire Abrahamic family; by the mystical visions of the orient, by stupendous Hindu dramas of our hidden heights and by the Buddha's grand desire that even the blades of the grass should be enlightened.

When I was a student at Stanford in the early eighties nothing exhilarated me more than the God-given diversity of the men and women living along my corridor in an ecumenically higgledy piggledy high-rise. Bahais taught me to launder in the basement utility; a Hindu shared her scriptures in MacDonald's; Orthodox twentysomethings spoke of the eucharistic prayers of Saint John Chrysostom, while my Filipino flatmate's wok steamed in the galley kitchen; Jews hung a mezuzah near the spyhole in their door; moslems glossed the newsprint copy on the holy city of Qum; courteous deists shook their bobble caps crossly over philandering weekly communicants, and the Marxists imagined that their Jewish prophet's messianic utopia would be in place, its totalitarian austerity over, by the stroke of midnight at the common era's millennium.

When am I going to learn that I can learn to go? Go see, go tell, go walkabout. When am I going to learn that the difference which makes the difference is difference itself?

Jesus is taken down from the Cross and buried
When I was small it seemed to me and to those who minded me that the natural dramatic climax of the Stations of the Cross occurred at the tenth halt, under the androgynous repose of the moment of death. Actually my prayers often skipped or at least undersubscribed the remaining panels of the epilogue to the pageant because they were actions of mechanical etiquette only on the part of the grieving bereaved. Deposition and burial were women's work, the finicky etcetera of the heroic holocaust.

Now I know different. Perhaps it's because I've waked a parent and woken to a child, perhaps it's because I've watched bloody life burst into the world between straining thighs or because the death throes of those who have gone before me, all shining and sweaty, resemble the birth pangs of the speechless babies who have battered with their fists in the birth canal; or maybe it's the life I've followed and sometimes tried to lead, a life of footsteps and trespasses, a sum of mucous membranes, some torn and unitary thing, an atom of psychosynthesis in a pitch-black body. Whatever the answer, the taking down of the circumcised alien from the glistening telegraph pole, the slotting of his rigidified limbs into an alcove full of geckoes, and the blundering insertion of the capstone – the last to be flung at him: the stone of lapidation, the stone of Sisyphus – to stop the orifice of the hole from gaping like a mouth, are images that imagine me. They are not the prestige pictures of Golgotha and Easter morning with their rhetoric of ruin and risenness. They are, instead, a muted, intermediate presence, the cigarette cards of no man's land. They are neither one thing nor another. They are neither here nor there.

They are the vigil matchsticks of Holy Saturday, the Sabbath itself.

Most of my friends and many of my contemporaries inhabit, as I do, that difficult, hospitable space between the end and the beginning again, between the sediments of failure and the fires of hope. They live in a quiet aftermath, in a posthumous listening. They know what it means to die and to descend to the dead. They know that it takes place. They know that it takes time. Not that my generation – old altarboys marrying in the sunlit registry office, the flower girls of the Corpus Christi conga scenting it all again in the slipstream of a toilet freshener – are hard pressed. We're not proteges of Amnesty in a breeze-block camp or women walking through a heat-haze with a petrol can for water. Onions make us cry, not tear gas. If we leave our medication in the powder room, one of the waitresses will bring it. This is not the stuff of the Sunday intercessions.

And yet there is a suffering people out there in the bright commuter shadowlands. Their sacredness is a shyness too. It is shy of the very sacramentality which names it. Heartbreak has made this people as human as Christ. In the stamina of their patience they are only divine. They will plant the grave tomorrow. They will change their hairstyle for starters. They will not drive by the school entrance any longer. They will let the children decide if he is the right person. They will cut their fathers' toenails the next time they take him out. They will wear the right sportsjacket for the second-stage interview. They will search on their hands and knees for the half a tablet from the blister foil.

And none of these women and men are asking for too much. They do not want to do as Thomas did. They do not want to grope at the body of love with their caterpillar fingers, parting and peering, prudish, empirical, in the male way, the phallic way, the possessive way. They are not the quantity surveyors of mystery, the proprietors of otherness. They would rather stand in a graveyard like Mary Magdalen and let the stinging antiseptic of their tears irrigate the ground beneath them until it greened gorgeously into the colours of chlorophyll, the flowering of a garden, and they heard themselves called by their own name for the first time in their life.

When am I going to?

From Ballybeg to London:
Worship and Sacrament Today

Michael Drumm

In Brian Friel's play *Dancing at Lughnasa* we encounter the life of the Mundy sisters who lived in Ballybeg, County Donegal in the 1930s. The story is very simple. It is the festival of Lughnasa, a pre-Christian celebration of the first fruits of the harvest in early August when people gather on hills and at wells to eat, drink and dance because the earth has yielded its fruit. But in the Mundy household all is not well because the older sister, Kate, objects to any vestige of pagan rituals and worse, her uncle, Fr Jack, has just been sent home after a lifetime in Uganda because of his participation in the pre-Christian traditions of the people among whom he worked. The only release from these tensions is in dancing, when the sisters appear to transcend their limited world. But the aching question remains – is this really transcendence or pure escapism, as in the end, despite the joy of the dance, two of the sisters are forced by economic circumstances to emigrate to London where they die in the loneliness of urban anonymity. The play might be understood as an elegy for the loss of a simple rural lifestyle in the face of the onslaught of modern economic forces, as the recent film production of the drama tends to do. But it is much more than that. It is a sustained reflection on realities that impinge upon us all at one time or another: the romantic allure of primitive rituals, the journey from childhood make-believe to adult reality, the clash of pagan traditions with Christian orthodoxy, the power of music and dance, the loneliness of the city, the human need for symbols and rituals which open up new horizons beyond the routine ordinariness of life. As human consciousness travels from Ballybeg to London, important issues are raised for Christian celebration and worship: will it disappear in the city? is it doomed to remain in Ballybeg and become nothing more than a part of nostalgic folklore? or can it begin to breathe anew even in the midst of the urban sprawl?

There is no simple solution to the problems posed by sacramental practice in today's church. In the Western world, technological and social changes continue at an extraordinary pace. Religious practice appears to satisfy the personal desires of some but is largely irrelevant in the overall scheme of things. It is being forced slowly but surely out of the public forum of arts, culture and new ideas and into the private realm of personal whim and choice. Its cultural underpinnings have collapsed as the mindset of the modern city supplants that of the primitive village. Not that all people used to live in villages or now live in cities, but the consciousness typical of one has replaced the other. Even if one lives in a rural area one's cultural consciousness is now that of the city, transported as it is by television to even the most remote locations. Not to live in accord with the implicit values and expectations of the city demands a very definite personal choice to opt out. Such an option will have radical social, economic and domestic implications as one is forced to live on the margins of society.

The village (alternatively one might call it the tribe or primitive society) had many attractions. Not least, people knew that they belonged. The meanings of the symbols and rituals that characterised their lives were certain. If someone called them into question, that person would have to leave, if not physically, then at least emotionally. As the people of the village world literally move into the modern world – the world of industry, mass education and the city – their traditional rituals are opened to question and often to ridicule. Slowly but surely many people begin to drift away from the rituals that were obligatory in the earlier society. These rituals were classically rites of passage associated with cosmic or biological passages; you could not be a part of the particular society without participating in these rituals for it was exactly through them that one was incorporated into the society. Throughout the world, people leave their tribal or village context for varied reasons; most are forced to move by the power of economic market forces, while some want to leave in order to escape the deadening ritualism of primitive societies as the rituals atrophy and decay. Those who are forced to leave as economic migrants at first cling on to their rituals but, through a process of ridicule, social conformism and the need for an economically more efficient lifestyle, they slowly abandon these earlier rites until they become just a part of folk memory. Yet for both of these groups, the economic migrants and those who wanted to escape, the need for ritual does not disappear but is expressed in new ways.

Ritual expression in today's world is different from that in the earlier societies in one key respect: the latter is characterised by obligation, the former by choice. Furthermore, ritual behaviour tends to migrate into the private world of individuals where it is linked with leisure time activities which do not detract from one's economic efficiency. The traditional rituals of primitive society fostered a strong sense of communal identity and bequeathed the symbols and values of the group to the next generation. As the efficacy of these rites declines, nothing sacred is communicated and so modern people freely choose other ways to express the life of the spirit. They do so through music and drama, theatre and film, literature and sport, and increasingly through consciousness-raising techniques and depth psychology. These then become the rituals of modernity; notice some of their key characteristics:

participation is voluntary and during one's free time, and the experience is normally private as the participants retreat very quickly to their homes or apartments without any great sense of communal identity having been created. These contrasts with primitive rituals are important but the ultimate contrast is this: modern people can wear the masks, prepare the special foods, engage in the dance, paint their faces, tell the stories, go to the hallowed place and so on, but they do so with a different consciousness, for we can never encounter the earth or the other world or the dead or the gods or our ancestors in the way that the participants in primitive rituals did.

We can never go home to the place of our ancient forbears nor can we ritualise as they did, but we can venture to the borderlands and whilst there hope to reap something of their wisdom and heritage. Some claim that the only way we as modern people can retrieve the rituals of primitive societies is through drama and music; that we erect a sacred space in our secular world called a theatre and only within it can we revisit the sacred spaces of earlier generations. In *Dancing at Lughnasa* the communal identity experienced on occasion amongst the family in Ballybeg is replaced by the bleak anonymity of the urban diaspora where two of the sisters disappear and die destitute. All of us must journey from Ballybeg to the city but the great danger is that we lose our identity in the process. No simple solution to this modern problem is available. Music and dance are potent forces for kindling the imagination, but religious ritual also offers the possibility of celebrating memory in a way that enriches the soul and nourishes identity. On the journey from Ballybeg to London, only memory and hope can save us. Religious rituals, with their sensitivity to the sacred and the archaic, should awaken a sense of these realities. Here are some pointers that might help them to do so.

Celebrating creation and redemption

Christianity is an awe-inspiring tradition of worship of the one true God before whom we bow rather than reason. But maybe we reason too much. Our church rituals are too cerebral and verbal. As we participate in these ancient practices we must be creative. Archaism and creativity go hand in hand. We must tap the ancient wellsprings of word and symbol, music and dance, art and movement, if people are to hear the Christian word. Many believers are turning to what is called 'creation-centred spirituality' in order to ritually express their faith anew. They are doing so because, quite literally, they find it more creative in terms of atmosphere, silence, movement and expression in celebrating the sacred. In today's television world, dominated as it is by Anglo-American television culture, we must face serious questions about how we will ritualise God's presence in our midst. Traditional Christian worship is centred on the redemption wrought by Christ. Today we need a renewed focus on the beauty and wonder of creation and on how this might be integrated into our religious rituals. Maybe we should compose new rites which celebrate the cycle of the seasons, the land, the harvest, personal development, the discovery of the indwelling God, the endless horizons of the inner life, the social and political demands of the gospel. The more creatively we celebrate these realities the more likely it is that people will indeed hear an echo of God's Spirit in their lives. But we need to take care here and not fool ourselves into thinking that simply celebrating creation will solve all of our problems.

The two most interesting contemporary examples of creation-centred spirituality are new ageism and, what has come to be known as 'Celtic spirituality'. Both have rather dubious credentials. They are in real danger of succumbing to the great temptation of our time – the belief that we can return to an earlier, more innocent age. In the same way that an adult can never become a child, so the children of the modern and post-modern worlds can never revert to the innocence of a bygone age. In suggesting that we can, these contemporary spiritualities are not nourishing the life of the soul but belittling the trauma that faces us. The task of celebrating both creation and redemption will not be facilitated by a romantic return to the past but by a courageous tussle with the key realities of our lives – grace and sin, friendship and loneliness, hope and despair, life and death. Only through this struggle will we learn what it means to be redeemed, and only when we have a sense that redemption is necessary and possible will sacrament and worship be truly meaningful.

Tasting transcendence
All of the cosmos is holy ground, but we need to erect sacred spaces to awaken us to this reality. Some of the greatest buildings in the world – the Pantheon and St Peter's Basilica in Rome, Hagia Sophia in Istanbul, the Dome of the Rock in Jerusalem – open up a space in which we can encounter the transcendent, since they are big enough to include all, high enough to awaken a sense of otherness and yet small enough to remind us that we need the community to accompany us on our pilgrim way. But whatever of these architectural gems, we all have need of holy places in our own lives, sanctuaries to which we can withdraw in order to get a different perspective on things. Without such spaces we are likely to degenerate into little more than automatons. As ever, we have much to learn from primitive societies. In the celebration of fertility rites, certain places were all important because they heightened the consciousness of participants of the fertility of the earth. The classic centres for such rituals were the mountain top and the well and, as a result, these became sacred places. In the case of mountains or hills, the height was not important but rather the breadth of the view over the sur-

rounding area as this awakened a sense of the beauty and fertility of the earth. Wells are sacred in all pre-modern societies as water is the most important gift that the earth provides. Similarly, pilgrimage centres, uninhabited islands, the seafront and monasteries became retreats from quotidian pre-occupations. These places are thresholds from which we can view life in a different way from the norm, where there is the possibility of encountering the immeasurable and transformative forces of the unconscious and the sacred. Ordinary life is routine, functional and often tedious. But the one-dimensional preoccupations of everyday life can be blown away by the awe-someness of the mountain-top; its predictability washed away by the ever changing power of the ocean; its noise quietened in the silence of the cloister or the church; its emptiness filled by the solitude of the island; its loneliness embraced in the encounter with fellow pilgrims; its finiteness questioned by the endless gurgling of new waters from the well. All of us need such experiences to nourish the life of the spirit.

These are some of the places which might give us a sense of transcend-ence, of otherness. But there are also people who, by their life choices, throw the cosy certainties of the majority of us into question. These people like liv-ing on the edge without order or structure and can happily accept chaos, insecurity, poverty and lack of social identity. You find them indulging in the craziest of adventures – climbing mountains best left alone, crossing seas in vessels more suited to ponds, hitching around the world instead of armchair travelling, renouncing a comfortable lifestyle to live amongst the poorest of the poor. We all desire to experience something of the grandeur of the moun-tain top, the awesomeness of the ocean, the detachment of the hitcher, the freedom of the one who chooses poverty over comfort. But we know that the cost involved is great and so we shy away from such a demanding lifestyle. Yet the encounter with life on the edge, the periphery, the margins remains the key to unleashing the powers of renewal in the lives of individuals and in the lives of great institutions like the churches. Creativity emerges from the margins. Artists, writers, philosophers, mystics go to the edge, the margins of their experience, and from there they interrogate the presumptions upon which our world is built. Christian worship needs to be challenged by such voices so that it does not descend into being little more than a prop for the dominant values and symbols of a particular society.

Abandoning magic, building community
Magic is the great temptation for all participants in ritual acts. Such magic makes people instruments rather than subjects of their own history; people go in search of security and special powers which are only accessible through particular rites. Such an approach robs people of their responsibility for

themselves and for others. It suggests that there is another way, a magical way, through which one can control the future. Magic lifts one out of the profane world into a sacred sphere wherein one can harness, for one's own benefit, strange powers not normally accessible. The only access to this sacred realm is through particular rites and rituals: through them we become part of a sacred world; without them we are lost in a profane world. One might schematise this as follows:

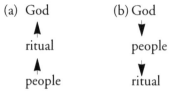

Scheme (a) represents a magical understanding as it suggests that the people only become sacred through participation in certain ritual acts. In other words the ritual is more important than the people as it is the ritual which is holy and opens the door to the sacred sphere; such a conception turns the participants in the ritual into instruments rather than subjects of their own history; instead of awakening them to a renewed sense of community and responsibility, it robs them of their true dignity in making them dependent on, and probably very fearful of, strange powers and dominations.

Scheme (b) represents a very brief and accurate outline of Christian history. Christians believe that God in Christ transformed everything human into something radically sacred, making them God's own people who then celebrate and deepen their identity through various rituals. Notice how central the communal dimension is in this scheme of things; rituals do not provide magical access to divine powers but rather God has created a people, a community, in which sacred rites ceaselessly affirm and challenge its true identity. This is what it means to move from magic to community, from abandoning ourselves to strange powers to embracing responsibility for our present and our future. All of this can be summarised in one principle: the people are primordial, the rituals are secondary.

During Christian sacramental worship, we need to foster a sense in which people are consciously present to one another in a way that doesn't happen on a train or in a supermarket or in a traffic jam or at a bar. The liturgical assembly must be retrieved from the clutches of an all too private form of piety, as if it were an occasion when I go to sort out my affairs with my God in much the same way as I deal individually with my lawyer or my doctor or my hairdresser or my garage mechanic. The church gathering must be different in creating a sense of belonging and shared responsibility. The church does not exist primarily for the spiritual comfort of individuals but rather to build a community that witnesses to the values of the Reign of God that Jesus preached. In trying to reform and renew our rituals, we will have to eradicate any vestiges of magic because being a disciple today will invariably mean being challenged to embrace responsibility for the future. Christian worship today will have to open people to the mysterious, awakening a sense of what is unseen and linguistically inexpressible, stirring the great powers of wonder and awe, creating small dynamic communities where people feel wanted and cared for, whilst affirming and challenging commitment.

Cherishing memory and hope

On the road from Ballybeg to London there is no return; this is a one-way ticket. On this journey religious rituals and worship should affirm and challenge us. If these rituals fail us then we could easily be lost in the anonymity of forgetfulness and despair. In the broken, messy world that we inhabit, celebrating Christian ritual is like erecting a sign that speaks of memory and hope. The two most important things that an individual ever says are: 'I remember' and 'I promise'. When these words lose their meaning, life unravels as our links with the past and the future are severed. People cannot survive long in such a vacuum – they will turn to fashion or drugs or ambition or suicide to numb the pain in facing an intolerable future. Our lives take shape in the space opened up between memory and hope. Memory gives us a sense of who we are and hope ceaselessly challenges us to renounce our self and sectional interests in an effort to construct a new future. Without memory and hope we are only scraps of biology blown hither and thither. On our passage from womb to tomb, we need symbols and rituals to keep hope and memory alive.

Occupying a Precarious Position: Women in Culture and Church in Ireland

Linda Hogan

In her prose memoir *Object Lessons,* Eavan Boland warns that we should not substitute the easy answer for the long haul. 'I see no redemption whatsoever,' she says, 'in moving from one simplification to the other.'[1] She is referring here to an overly simplistic feminist reading of the history of women's exclusion from the poetic tradition. However, her caution has wider purchase beyond the realm of poetry and the arts. In the context of feminist analyses of Christianity, and in particular Roman Catholicism, her admonition is especially pertinent. It reminds one that the past cannot be read as one continuous patriarchal betrayal of women by men. Moreover, it suggests that a future cannot be imagined without confronting the reality that women as well as men have colluded in and extended patterns of oppression and violence. In contemplating recent decades of feminist critique of the Christian tradition, what strikes me most is that although feminism has given us a partial understanding of the structures of domination, we are still struggling to comprehend the complexities of power and the way it infuses all our relationships and institutions. Women and men both have occupied ambiguous and often precarious positions within patriarchy, and feminism has had an important role in theorising this. However, feminism must take care to avoid construing women primarily as victims and men as victors. This is especially the case in relation to the Roman Catholic Church, which on a superficial reading could be interpreted this way.

Of course I do a disservice to feminism in suggesting that it is not sufficiently aware of the complexities of power relations and the role of women in their perpetuation. Feminism has long been cognisant of this. However, it has also been guilty of speaking in clichés, portraying women only as victims and promoting the facile hope that, if women had a greater role to play, society would be more just and caring. In fact feminism's own past points to a far more intricate and subtle relationship between women men and power. The reality of feminist politics, both in the late nineteenth and twentieth centuries suggests that women are not the great innocents of history and that relationships between women do not necessarily proceed on the basis of mutuality and care. Women too struggle to embody such values in our relationships,

---

1. *Object Lessons,* Vintage, 1995, p 244.

both personal and political. Indeed it is my firm conviction that if feminism is to flourish in the next century it will need to divest itself of the myth of female victimhood and of a simplistic vision of global sisterhood.

In Ireland women's position with regard to both church and society embodies many of these ambiguities. One reading of the political history of both church and state would relegate women to the periphery, would regard women to be 'outside history'. In many respects women could be said to be absent from the collective public memory of our history, and when they are present it is often as tokens, interlopers or oddities. Our understanding of the true extent of women's involvement in the creation of contemporary Ireland is in some measure corrected by the retrieval of the memory of the politically and religiously significant women who have been written out of history. Feminist scholars have highlighted the significance of women like Anne Devlin, compatriot of Robert Emmet, Countess Markievicz, Eva Gore-Booth, Catherine Macaulay and Margaret Aylward, who in their different ways were politically influential. Similarly the heritage of Irish women artists, poets and intellectuals is being recovered. The fragile worlds of the astronomer and microscopist Mary Ward, of the novelist Maria Edgeworth, and of artists Mary Delany and Mainie Jellet, who pursued their craft against the tide of history and social convention, suggest an account of women's involvement in the shaping of modern Ireland that cannot be understood as merely passive.

Yet it is fair to say that on balance women have been, and continue to be excluded from the centres of decision-making and influence. Undoubtedly women have made significant strides in some fields. In medicine, in politics, in the financial sector and in the academy, women are present in far greater numbers than ever before. It must be acknowledged, however, that even in these arenas women continue to be under-represented in their higher echelons. Women's contribution to the renaissance in the arts too is an indication of their growing public presence. However, beyond the professional lives of some women it is questionable whether the lot of women, especially of poor women, has improved substantially. True there are fewer instances of overt discrimination. Women can now play their part as full citizens of the republic, can serve on juries, can continue in their jobs after marriage and are treated as adults by the bureaucratic arm of the state. There is also less tolerance of domestic violence and of abuse of various kinds. Yet the devastating poverty and violence that characterises the lives of many women, men and children stands as a corrective to the optimistic story of untrammelled progress which often goes unchallenged.

The feminist critique of the Christian tradition

Feminist challenges to the political system eventually began to be felt within religious traditions also. This is true of all the major world religions, but is especially true of Christianity in the Western world. Mirroring feminism's interaction with other fields, feminist theology arose out of the recognition that the Christian tradition has radically excluded the experiences of women from the articulation of its beliefs, values and practices. From the 1960s on, a number of Christian women including Kari Borressen, Mary Daly and Rosemary Radford Ruether began to identify and critique the many ways in which the Christian tradition created and perpetuated the marginality of women, both in the churches and in society. This involved a gendered analysis of biblical and theological texts in order to reveal the misogynistic assumptions beneath many of the doctrines and traditions of Christianity. The study of what Phyllis Trible called the 'texts of terror', those texts in which women are vilified, cursed, shunned and degraded, has formed an important part of feminist theological reflection. Accounts of woman as 'the devil's gateway' (Tertullian), as 'a misbegotten male' (Aquinas), or as 'not the image of God save in her capacity as helpmate' (Augustine) abound in the classic texts of the Christian tradition. And although they may now be rejected as unimportant vestiges of an age long past, feminists have insisted that their legacies endure in the institutionalised sexism of the contemporary Christian churches.

The Catholic Church's refusal to recognise that women as well as men may have a vocation to the ministerial priesthood is a potent symbol of this persistent sexism. This sexism is seen also in the fact that virtually all the teaching offices of the Catholic Church are occupied by men, even though the formal teaching offices need not necessarily be held by clerics. The downgrading of female images for God, images that are evident in the symbolic tradition of Catholicism, is yet another instance of institutionalised sexism. The predominance of the father image in the contemporary God-language of Christianity also creates the false impression that the Christian God can be adequately and exclusively understood as male. This focus on just one of the many images used in the biblical texts has led to the exclusion of the rich and potent symbolism of biblical, patristic and medieval theology and spirituality from our contemporary religious consciousness. These and many other deeply ingrained patterns of thought and practice contribute to the sense that many women and men have that Christianity in its many forms is inherently sexist and patriarchal.

Much of the initial scrutiny of the Christian tradition through the lens of gender occurred in the United States and in Britain. Once they had access to theological training and scholarship many women became conscious of the sexism that is part of the tradition. The Christian churches in Ireland have

also been subject to similar, if not identical criticisms, and theologians working in Ireland have been to the fore in drawing attention to these problems.
Indeed this growth in feminist consciousness among women and men has
truly transformed the shape of theological scholarship in this country over
the past two decades. Influential thinkers and practitioners, such as Mary
Condren, Katherine Zappone, Ann-Louise Gilligan, Ben Kimmerling, Anne
Thurston, Enda McDonagh and Dermot Lane, to mention just a few, have
given voice to the deep alienation generated by participation in destructive
structures of thought and practice. But their analysis has not ended with critique. They and many others have also contributed to the discussion about
alternative, liberative ways of being spiritual persons within a community of
believers.

The critique of Christianity's sexist past has occasioned many debates
about the ethical viability of Christianity and about whether women's spiritual future should lie within or outside the borders of traditional religion.
Many women have joined Mary Daly in her exodus from patriarchal religion,[2]
and have understood it as an exodus from alienated relationship. Others have
been similarly determined to journey from alienated relationship, but believe
that this can be done within the church, through the transformation of the
institutional patterns that deform the spirit of Christianity. Those feminists
who have remained (marginally) within the tradition have been adamant that
no less than a complete paradigm shift is necessary if Christianity is to be a
vehicle of spiritual growth and liberation for both women and men. Indeed
much of the work of feminist theology since the 1960s, both in the academy
and in the wider community, has been focused on identifying the elements
that will facilitate a change of consciousness and effect this paradigm shift.

Women's experience as a source of religious insight
One of the most subversive aspects of feminist theology has been its insistence on writing women's experience into the centre of theological reflection.
This has involved drawing on women's experience both as a source of religious understanding as well as an important component in the evaluation of
the spiritual value of the tradition. Undoubtedly this has been a source of
controversy, with opponents of feminist theology insisting that feminists
import an inappropriate subjectivism and politicism into religion. However,
as Rosemary Radford Ruether argues in her *Sexism and God-Talk,* those elements that have been called the objective sources of theology, that is scripture

---

2. In 1971 the theologian and philosopher of religion Mary Daly preached a famous sermon
during a Sunday service at Harvard University. During her sermon she invited the women and
men present to join her in an exodus from the church, which many did. They enacted it sym-
bolically that day by pouring out into Harvard Yard, thus making history.

and tradition, are themselves codified collective human experience.[3] Religion, according to Ruether, is constituted in a hermeneutical circle of past and present experiences, with scripture and tradition being the expression and memory of the past. Religious traditions begin to be shaped when the community appropriates these revelatory experiences. These experiences are then categorised, invested with authority and ultimately mediated through narratives, symbols and rituals. What makes feminist theology distinctive in Ruether's eyes, is not that it imports a subjective element into the interpretation of religious meaning, because all religion does this, but that it imports the experience of those whose voice has long been silenced, that is of women. This understanding of the nature of religious traditions does not deny the significance of revelatory experiences, however it insists that all revelatory experiences are mediated through past cultural symbols and traditions, which in turn are experiences that have been collectively moulded by a formative group.

The formative groups through history have tended to be the religious elites, those teachers, preachers and functionaries who have had access to scholarship and learning. Thus the construction and interpretation of church doctrines, the articulation of ethical frameworks, the crafting of symbol systems, in fact all that constitutes the substance of religion, all of this emerges out of the dialectic of collective religious experience. This way of understanding religious traditions is not specifically feminist, but it does explain the absence of a female voice in the shaping of Christianity as well as indicate a future role for women's experience in the articulation of that tradition. Feminist theology's insistence that women's experience should be central to the interpretative process that constitutes religion is highly significant because it resituates religious authority and suggests a different model of power. As a result, religion is no longer conceived in terms of an almighty God revealing himself to a chosen few, but in terms of the experience of the divine infusing one's religious imagination and thereby shaping the collective life and worship of the community.

This process of imagining an alternative religious consciousness, one that is rooted in the texts and traditions of Christianity, but understood in a different register, has been the major work of feminist theology in the last three decades. Of course there were glimpses of such alternative visions in earlier centuries, however this process has gained momentum in recent decades. The legitimacy of forging different symbol systems and ethical frameworks is underwritten by this recognition that existing patterns of thought too are the product of interpreted experience. Such a perspective allows for the possibil-

---

3. R. Ruether, *Sexism and God-Talk: Towards a Feminist Theology*, London: SCM, p 12.

ity that at certain times inherited patterns of thought and symbolic practices may no longer illuminate contemporary religious experience. Indeed this is precisely what has happened within the Christian tradition in the past three or four decades. Many women and men recognised that there is a contradiction between received images, interpretations and values on the one hand, and their experiences of grace and redemption on the other. And it is in this gap between received interpretations of religious truth that the sacred is currently being refigured.

The limitations of women's experience

Yet even as Christian feminist women were protesting at the exclusionary practices of the institutional church and the absence of women's voice, feminists themselves were coming under attack from women whose perspective was not represented by feminism. Thus began a long and painful learning process in which many feminists recognised that they had replicated one of the most oppressive features of patriarchal thought, in assuming that all women share a common experience and in presuming to speak for all women. African-American women were initially to the fore in reminding white middle-class women that they had essentially whitewashed women's experience and been blind to the racism and poverty that shapes the experiences of many women. Feminists have thus come to recognise that women's experience is extremely varied and fractured and that women do not share a uniform material reality. Furthermore, feminism worldwide has begun to acknowledge that there are serious inequalities of power between women, with many women making 'bargains' with the powerful institutions and thus benefiting from belonging to a particular racial, ethnic or economic group. The politics of feminism in South Africa since the 1960s highlights the complex and often fraught nature of the power that women wield. Moreover, it suggests that a simple gender analysis is inadequate to the task of truly coming to terms with the nature and extent of patriarchal power in society.

Women and power

In both the secular and religious contexts in Ireland there is still a tendency to promote the kind of analysis which ignores the extent of the power and influence that women actually hold and which disregards the conflicts that exist between women. In the United States these issues have been frequently debated and much of the analysis is particularly instructive. Since the beginning of the feminist movement in the nineteenth century, in the United States the history of white women's participation in the culture of slavery has been a contentious issue. The fact that hundreds of thousands of white women colluded with and worked for the enforcement of the savagery of slavery challenges received ideas of women as innocent onlookers in a political system not of their making. Whereas it is true that women did not have a direct role in constructing and maintaining the political machinery of slavery, they did play a significant part in its perpetuation. One example of the numerous ways in which white women co-operated in this is recorded by Stanley Feldstein who tells of an incident in which a plantation owner was discovered raping a thirteen-year-old slave girl. His wife's rage was directed at the child who was flogged daily for several weeks.[4] Moreover the realisation that white women benefited directly from the brutalisation and demonisation of black women further complicates the picture.

A number of the slave narratives of the nineteenth century record the 'patriarchal bargain' which white women made during the years of slavery. In addition, the fiction of many contemporary African-Americans like Toni Morrison help to unravel the complex manner in which gender and race intersect. In Ireland we do not live directly with the heritage of slavery, but the dynamics of power and the various positions of women within the web of unequal relationships which slavery reveals is relevant in this context also. One only has to think of the rigidly stratified society of Ireland in the 1950s to recognise the deep divisions that existed among women and the way in which the respectability of some women was bought at the expense of others. For example, the attitude to and treatment of unmarried mothers reveals a great deal about both the powerlessness of some women and the powerfulness of others. In her novel *Down by the River*, Edna O'Brien has a wonderfully revealing vignette in which this is explored. Here she lays bare the various mechanisms by which the virtuous women in any society perpetuate elements of the misogyny for self-interest, and the way in which they throw in their lot with the patriarchy. It paints a picture of the patriarchal bargain in which women's own gendered subjectivities, together with their investment in particular relationships, work to maintain a delicate balance of power and to safeguard spheres of autonomy they already control.

We see the complex nature of women and power played out in many situations, but there is none more challenging than the role of religious women in running institutions in which children were systematically abused and brutalised. It is here that we come face to face with the inadequacy of simplistic analyses of patriarchy in which women are always cast as the powerless, voiceless victims. There is no doubt that women's collusion in deeply damaging practices can in part be explained by the internalisation of patriarchal values and by the attractions of the rewards that accrued to dutiful daughters. In the case of religious women, the years of formation in the virtues of modesty, passivity and self-abegnation have certainly taken their

---

4. Recounted in Bell Hooks' *Ain't I a Woman: Black Women and Feminism,* Boston: South End Press, 1981, p. 37.

toll. However, talk of colonisation and the internalisation of the patriarchal system cannot explain this away. In many respects, women gained in direct proportion to the support they gave to these institutions.

In my view, this situation can be best understood as an instance of structural sin. This phrase refers to the fact that we live in a social environment that bears the marks of failure. Our social, cultural and religious context often functions to obscure value and to hinder our moral development. Our sense of value is tied up with the community to which we belong and the social context in which we live. This context often functions in a negative manner, hiding values, giving priority to inessentials, or desensitising us to particular injustices. The fact that these biases are hidden in ideologies and reinforced in many different cultural assumptions and patterns of behaviour means that we are often unaware of our participation in social sin. As a result, the biases and blindness of the prevailing cultural ethos limit the extent to which one can make personal moral decisions.

However, although we may be caught in a web of structural sin and of systemic failure, we can never avoid the issue of personal responsibility. The Christian tradition is built on the assumption that although social and cultural practices play an important role in shaping our sense of morality, they do not determine it. We do have a sort of freedom that enables us to evaluate, and then either reject or endorse the dominant culture. Social embodiment is important, but not decisive, in the individual's pursuit of good.

Refiguring the dynamics of power

The history of Catholicism in twentieth-century Ireland has been radically rewritten in the 1990s with the truth about the church's role in maintaining such a brutal system being told. Indeed this changes completely and forever our received understandings and interpretations of 'Catholic Ireland'. The relentless revelations of abuse indicate that our theological and religious heritage needs to be re-evaluated. The degree to which women as well as men invested their bodies and souls in these abusive institutions requires us to rethink the religious and moral formation that underlay and sustained such practices. We desperately need a systematic analysis of the various positions that men and women, religious and lay adopted, together with an investigation of the underlying theology. The truth will inevitably be ambiguous and multi-layered, with prevarication and accommodation as well as resistance being part of the story. What is clear, however, is that an overly monolithic conception of male dominance will obfuscate rather than reveal the complex dynamics of power that characterises human relationships.

Feminist theology has long been critical of the destructive models of power together with the over-spiritualisation of persons and values that enabled these institutions and practices to flourish. Although it did focus initially on issues of women's exclusion, feminist theology has expanded both its analysis and its horizons in order to respond to all forms of dominance. In this, feminist theology has been part of a collective determination on the part of many Christians to transform our received understandings of the tradition. On account of this, the centre of gravity of feminist theology is changing, with attention being given to the complex web of violence and domination that is suffused through social and cultural life. Of course it is not that gender is unimportant but that the gendered construction of social roles and symbolic practices is but one of a number of factors that create systems of oppression. As a result, the church's response to the situation of women cannot be seen apart from its day to day struggle to enact the values of the gospel and to embody the Christian vision and vocation in the social context.

There are many people within the Christian tradition in Ireland who are working to create a new religious space and who are part of a fragile and somewhat haphazard coalition for renewal. Feminist theological analysis has contributed significantly to this process and continues to do so as its sense of the dynamics of power evolves and becomes more subtle. If the church is to have a future then it will need to contribute to our sense of human flourishing, facilitate the promotion of relationships of mutuality and trust and partake of the collective endeavour to envision and enact institutions of co-responsibility. The insights of feminist theology are vital to this task, not as an addendum, but as an integral component of both the critique and the reconstruction.

Christian Values in a Pluralist Society

Patrick Hannon

A few years ago the title of this paper would probably have suggested a reflection on morality and law in the context of church-state relations in Ireland, and the church most prominently in question was the Roman Catholic. For we had grown accustomed to recurrent public debate about the embodiment of certain moral beliefs in the law of the land, and the focal question usually was whether it was appropriate that, in an increasingly pluralist society, moral beliefs associated especially (and sometimes exclusively) with the Catholic Church should in effect be imposed on people not of that faith.

But most of the controversies of the past few decades have been settled: the 'special position' of the Catholic Church accorded by the Constitution – for what in any case it meant – is a dim memory, the laws which reflected Catholic teaching on contraception have gone, and there is no longer a constitutional prohibition on divorce legislation.[1] And the potential for influence of the leadership of the church has apparently been diminished, partly because of the scandals which have beset the church over the past decade, partly also because of the decline in church membership which appears to have taken hold during the same period, and to an increasingly evident pluralism of religious belief and practice.

So our title now bespeaks a different kind of reflection, or rather a reflection in different terms. For the question is no longer primarily that of the influence of the institutional church or churches upon the institutions of the state, but the influence of Christianity in the shaping of Irish society. I do not mean to say that the church as an institution can have no influence in that process; indeed I shall maintain later that it can and should. But the church is in the first place the community of believers in the way of the Lord Jesus. And it is through the life and activity of the members of that community that Christian values and the Christian vision for human living will be mediated to future generations.

---

1. Abortion is of course a critically important exception, and there has also been some public discussion of the law on euthanasia. A government Green Paper is being prepared at present which is expected to offer a range of proposals to deal with the legal situation created by the 'X' case. The response of the Bishops' Conference to any proposals concerning the law in these areas will be informed by the teaching of Pope John Paul's encyclical *Evangelium Vitae*. See especially paragraphs 68-74, tr. Veritas, Dublin 1995, pp 124-137.

It was inevitable, though also misleading, that the question should in the past have been framed in terms of church-state relations. It was inevitable because there were in fact discernible traces of Catholic influence in the Constitution of 1937 and in various legislation since the foundation of the state in 1922. And, on the whole, people were content to leave direction on moral questions to the leaders of the church, as they were law to the leaders of the state. It was, however, also misleading, for it masked the fact that at the core of each debate was an issue with which every society has to contend: how to reconcile individual freedoms with the claims of a common welfare. It tended to mask, too, the truth that responsibility for the moral future of Ireland lies in the conscience of every citizen of whatever religious persuasion.

There are advantages and opportunities in the changed situation. There is the challenge now of recognising that responsibility for the preservation of moral values lies not just with the leaders of the churches or of the state but with each citizen. There is an opportunity to take seriously the point that morality is concerned not just with a handful of issues of sexual ethics, but with the whole spectrum of our relationships with each other and with the world which we inhabit. At another level, we are coming to see that we are now part of the larger community of Europe, indeed of the world, and that our moral agenda is no longer merely domestic.

The challenges

More than thirty years ago the Second Vatican Council described the modern situation in terms whose truth has been endorsed by all that has happened since, and which remain an apt account of today's world: 'Ours is a new age of history with profound and rapid changes spreading gradually to all corners of the earth. They are the products of people's intelligence and creative activity, but they recoil upon them, upon their judgments and desires, both individual and collective, upon their ways of thinking and acting in regard to people and things. We are entitled then to speak of a real social and cultural transformation whose repercussions are felt at the religious level also.'[2] Advances in science and technology, all that is involved – economically, politically, socially, culturally – in 'globalisation', the persistence of warfare and the continuing threat of nuclear disaster, various threats to the environment, contexts and the background to choices and decisions which will determine the future of humanity and our world.

Ireland, for better and for worse, is in the mainstream of change now, and there is no issue of a global order which will not have an impact, direct or indirect, on us. The problems of 'Europe' – and so, also, the problems of the

---

2. *Gaudium et Spes,* par 4, tr A. Flannery (ed), *Vatican Council II. Constitutions, Decrees, Declarations,* Dublin and New York 1996.

world – are our problems in an unprecedented way. And we have some characteristic problems of our own. The most pressing still is the achievement of
a lasting peace on our island, with prospect of a real reconciliation, and the
creation of the social conditions in which each man and woman may be
assured of respect for their dignity as human beings. This is a task of politics
and of politicians, but is at its core a moral challenge, and responsibility for
it lies in the consciences of all the people of our island, however remotely
some of us may feel ourselves touched by the realities of the conflict in the
North.

There are other problems and challenges. The poor are still with us of
course, their plight the more striking now in the light of the prosperity of the
many and the great wealth of a few, and a recent UN report shows that we
have the second highest level of poverty in the industrialised world for the
second successive year. According to another UN report, almost a quarter of
the population is functionally illiterate. And with poverty and deprivation go
homelessness, loneliness, illness and suicide.

Not that Irish society has been oblivious of these defects, and during the
past few decades there have been renewed efforts on the part of the state to
alleviate poverty and to help cope with the problems to which poverty gives
rise. We have witnessed also a considerable improvement as regards access to
education at all levels, and there have been advances also in healthcare and in
the sphere of 'welfare', for all that there remains much to criticise. And we
have had an impressive contribution from voluntary organisations, whether
religious in their inspiration or secular, even when their best efforts are regularly frustrated through lack of funding and other resources.

But improvement is slow, change often not radical enough; and there is
evidence of a lack of political will when it comes to any measure which might
trouble the more powerful sectors of society.[3] There is evidence also of a
detachment – a growing detachment? – on the part of people generally from
the problems of those who are on the margins and who remain deprived. It
is disquieting to learn that organisations such as the St Vincent de Paul
Society and the Simon Community are having difficulty recruiting volunteers.

---

3. A majority of the Constitutional Review Group rejected the suggestion that economic and
social rights might be included in a revised Constitution: see *Report of the Constitution Review
Group,* May 1996, Government Publications, pp 234-236. There are obvious difficulties but
none that is obviously insuperable. The case for inclusion of rights to health, adequate housing, adequate nutrition and an adequate standard of living is argued in *Re-righting the
Constitution,* published in 1998 by the Irish Commission for Justice and Peace. This is the
product of a process which involved written and oral submissions to the All Party Committee
for the Review of the Constitution, and it includes a response to the main objections and difficulties raised in the Review Group's Report.

The Irish tradition has accorded a special place to hospitality and the kindly treatment of the stranger. It is again disconcerting to witness the ambivalence at an official level, and the hostility and resentment in some localities, in dealing with refugees and asylum-seekers during the past few years. Even more ominous are the reports of racist attitudes and reactions in the streets and in particular neighbourhoods. Tourists, expecting to be met with friendliness and courtesy – not to mention fair dealing and value for money – are latterly encountering obnoxious behaviour at the hands of their hosts. Some immigrants have a tale to tell which puts stark questions about our real attitudes to the stranger.[4]

There are issues which arise directly out of our participation in the forging of a European Union. We have been happy to accept the economic benefits which membership of the Union has brought, and on the whole our participation in the political and administrative structures of the Union has been creditable. But public consciousness of our membership is dominated by the motif of economic benefit, and it will be interesting to see how we react when, as is inevitable, economic benefit is not so immediate or obvious. During the past few years, voices have been heard among the Union's leaders recalling the vision of the founders, for whom economic co-operation, albeit crucial, was only the basis and starting-point for a social and political co-operation which betokened a real solidarity and a truly human community. It would be strange indeed if we were unable and unwilling to contribute to that task out of the resources bequeathed us by our history and our cultural and spiritual inheritance.

The Patrimony

Moral values are not abstract; they are embodied in the choices which people make, and these choices tell more about the actual value system of an individual or a people than do the formal or official accounts to which people profess to subscribe. The vision of life which we have inherited is predominantly Christian, but of course it does not follow that the values which have shaped and shape our choices are always the values of Christianity.

There is nothing surprising about this: 'For I do not do the good that I want, but the evil that I do not want is what I do.'[5] And our perceptions, as individuals or as a society, of 'the good that I want' are conditioned by time and place, and it is easier in hindsight to see fault and wrong than it is to know what to do in the present and for the future. The shortcomings of Irish

---

4. See, for example, Chichi Aniagolu, 'Being Black in Ireland', in Ethel Crowley and Jim MacLaughlin (eds), *Under the Belly of the Tiger: Class, Race, Identity and Culture in the Global Ireland*, Dublin 1997.

5. Rom 7:19. The translation used throughout is the New Revised Standard Version.

Christianity have been all too well documented in the media and in the novels and drama of our time, and it is salutary for Christians to reflect upon and repent, and where possible atone for, the sins of the past. But it is folly to suppose that the human propensity to do what is good, or our ability to discern what is truly good, is purer, less prone to error and to wilful failure, than was the case in past generations. Self-righteousness is never a good starting point for an attempt to discover and live better ways, and the demonising and scapegoating of individuals or of groups is both infantile and unproductive.

I have already made the point that responsibility for the future of moral values rests with each citizen of whatever religious persuasion. And Christians who wish to work for the moral betterment of society take their place along-side people of goodwill who do not share their faith. But Christians are entitled, and by their own faith obliged, to reflect upon the problems of today and tomorrow, in the light of the Christian moral patrimony.

What values do Christians profess to cherish, and must wish to pass on to the next generation? The Christian gospel is first a religious message: the kingdom of God – the reign of love and justice and grace and peace – has been inaugurated, and in the fulness of time God will be all in all. But this has direct implications for the moral life, the chief of which is that we are to love our neighbour as ourselves. And the neighbour is everyone, for we are each made in the image of God, and each is brother or sister in the Lord.

The simplicity of the love commandment is, of course, deceptive, for though some of its requirements are almost self-evident, and Christians see them as endorsed by Revelation – respect for life, truthfulness, giving people their rights, looking out for the neighbour in need – it is not always easy in practice to discern the concrete forms of behaviour to which these require-ments give rise. The essentials do not change, but the world which the fol-lowers of Jesus inhabit is diverse and changing. And the Christian tradition has grappled with these questions through the centuries, evolving principles and norms of behaviour which aim to embody the moral vision which Jesus taught and lived. The community of Christian believers has also tried to live up to that vision, or live it, sometimes successfully, sometimes not. And so it is with the community of Christians today.

Our time professes to place a special value on the dignity of the human being; and we speak also of equality, and of the value of freedom as a constit-utive element of human dignity. And we have come to speak of 'human rights' – entitlements which belong to everyone by virtue simply of being human, and which must be respected, and guaranteed and vindicated by the law. The Christian moral tradition is on the whole content to adopt the con-cept and the language of human rights in order to express the concrete demands of right moral living. It is aware of the danger of a certain individualist bias in rights discourse and in their pursuit, and seeks to counter it by an insistence on correlative responsibilities, and by emphasising the need to recognise that we are persons-in-community and the virtue of neighbourly solidarity.

In their commitment to notions such as human dignity and equality and in their recognition of the claims expressed as human rights, conscientious Christians can feel at one with conscientious people of other religions and of none. And they can make common cause with people not of their faith in the struggle to secure the human rights of those who are deprived of them. The church in the modern world can, as the Second Vatican Council put it, share the joy and hope as well as the grief and anguish of every man and woman of our time.[6] There are commonalities as well as pluralism of moral value, in Ireland as elsewhere, and the differences between (and among) Christians and others ought not to be exaggerated.

A specifically Christian contribution?

But can Christians bring anything in particular to the task of creating Ireland's future? During the past few decades there has been a debate among theologians as to what, if anything, differentiates the morality of Christian faith from that of other people. The debate has hinged upon the question whether there is anything in the content of Christian morality which cannot be discerned from a reasoned reflection on what it is to be a human being in the world. Contributors to the discussion are agreed that Christian faith furnishes a vision of life, within which we make our moral choices, and which influences the choices we make. It is also agreed that the Christian faith-vision offers a distinctive and enhanced motivation for moral living: a Christian professes to behave rightly toward the fellow human being not only because the other is equal in dignity but because he or she is brother or sister in the Lord. And all recognise the powerful exemplary significance of the way in which Jesus lived and died. The difference between them is on the question whether there are concrete norms of behaviour which can be known only from Revelation and in faith.

The detail of the debate and its present status needn't concern us here.[7] For our purposes it is perhaps enough to say this. Whatever the differences or commonalities between the morality of the Christian and that of others, the profession of Christianity in any case commits one to certain perspectives on human living, and it commits one to certain kinds of choices. The Christian believes in a creator-God, whose creation reflects the goodness and beauty of the divine, and of whom the human person is an image. And this

---

6. *Gaudium et Spes*, Preface.
7. See Vincent Macnamara, 'The Distinctiveness of Christian Morality' in Bernard Hoose (ed), *Christian Ethics*, London 1998, p 149 ff.

God is trinitarian, and the image of God in us is relational, so that in our deepest nature we are persons-in-community.

The Christian's picture of life includes an acknowledgement of sin and sinfulness, personal, social and structural. It does not minimise what is nowadays called the dark side of human nature and human existence. It acknowledges that at our best our motivations are mixed, our achievements imperfect, our best constructs flawed. But it trusts also in the hope of salvation, for the individual and for the world, which is disclosed in the death and resurrection of Jesus the Christ. And its focus upon Jesus as the Way, the Truth and the Life entails commitment to the love-commandment as it was taught and lived by him.

And in the disclosure of the dimensions of the love-commandment in the preaching and life of Jesus there is an unmistakable bias toward the neighbour who is in need – toward the people on the margins, as they are often called today. The tone is set in Luke's account of the beginning of Jesus' ministry in Galilee, as Jesus visits the synagogue of his youth and unrolls the scroll and finds where it is written: 'the Spirit of the Lord is upon me, because he has anointed me to bring the good news to the poor. He has sent me to proclaim release to the captives and recovery of sight to the blind, to let the oppressed go free, to proclaim the year of the Lord's favour.'[8] 'Today this scripture has been fulfilled in your hearing.'[9]

The impact and significance of Jesus' meeting with the woman at the well is underestimated if we are not aware of certain prejudices of his time and place.[10] The choice of a Samaritan as a model of neighbourly behaviour toward the man who fell among robbers had to be startling to an audience for whom the Samaritans were enemy.[11] The renunciation of any kind of temporal power and of coercion in the fulfilment of his destiny as Messiah was shocking to people who looked for political deliverance and an earthly kingdom. Jesus' acceptance of death on a cross was a scandal and a folly.[12]

It is not, therefore, a merely transient incident of contemporary Christianity that the faith of the Christian should impel to active concern for the poor, and to transformative action in aid of the dignity and equality and entitlement to their human rights of everyone, and especially of the people of the margins. In words of the Synod on Justice in the World in 1971: 'Action on behalf of justice and participation in the transformation of the world fully appear to us [the Pope and the bishops of the world gathered in

---

8. Lk 4:18,19.
9. Lk 4:22.
10. Jn 4:1-30.
11. Lk 10:25-37.
12. I Cor 1:23.

synod] as a constitutive dimension of the preaching of the Gospel, or, in other words, of the Church's mission for the redemption of the human race and its liberation from every oppressive situation.'[13] This is the consistent message also of the social teaching of Pope John Paul II.[14]

There is of course more to be said about the Christian understanding of the moral life than that it involves what is nowadays called a preferential option for the poor. One might, for example, speak of the radicality and generosity of moral response which is called for in the Sermon on the Mount.[15] One might reflect on the implications of the biblical concepts of morality as discipleship or as imitation of Christ. One might refer to the fact that in Christian theology 'to imitate and live out the love of Christ is not possible for man by his own strength alone. He becomes capable of this love only by virtue of a gift received.'[16] And one might raise the question of the relationship between Christian spirituality, including prayer and sacramental worship, and a conscious living out of the Christian moral vision.

But these themes are beyond the scope of this piece, the main concern of which is to suggest what, at least in general terms, adherents of the Christian tradition might contribute to promoting and sustaining moral value in Ireland in the new millennium. It is an important part of my case that responsibility rests with each Christian, and that the values of the gospel will be realised only insofar as they inform and inspire the decisions and choices which Christians make. But of course it may also be expected that the churches as institutions will continue to play a part. I am thinking mainly of my own church, so it is perhaps all the more necessary to make the point that common sense, not to mention their common commitment to the core values

13. *Justice in the World,* Synod of Bishops 1971, tr A. Flannery (ed), *Vatican Council II. More Post-Conciliar Documents,* Dublin 1982, p 696.

14. See especially *Centesimus Annus,* tr Veritas, Dublin 1991. In view of the context in which the present collection of essays is being presented it is especially interesting to read the second chapter of *Tertio Millenio Adveniente,* the Apostolic Letter in which the Pope deals with the Catholic Church's preparation for the millennium Jubilee. The chapter reflects upon the meaning of Jubilee, linking it with the passage in Luke 4 cited above, and suggesting that the social doctrine of the church is rooted in the tradition of the jubilee year. See esp. pars 11-13, tr CTS London 1994.

15. Mt 5-7. Cf. Lk 6, 11, 12. Commenting on the moral teaching of the Sermon, 'the *magna charta* of gospel morality', the present Pope has written: *'Jesus brings God's commandments to fulfilment,* particularly the commandment of love of neighbour, *by interiorising their demands and by bringing out their fullest meaning.* Love of neighbour springs from *a loving heart* which, precisely because it loves, is ready to live out *the loftiest challenges.* Jesus shows that the commandments must not be understood as a minimum limit not to be gone beyond, but rather as a path involving a moral and spiritual journey towards perfection, at the heart of which is love (cf. Col 3:14).' *Veritatis Splendor,* par 15, tr as in John Wilkins (ed), *Understanding Veritatis Splendor,* London 1994, pp 94, 95. Original emphasis.

16. op. cit. p 101.

of the Christian message, suggests that the time is ripe for exploring ways in which the Christian churches might co-operate among themselves in the task of shaping the Ireland of the future.

Church and society in the future
The dimensions of the changes which have been taking place in the Catholic Church in Ireland during the past decade are not yet fully clear, nor is their full significance for the task of leadership in the church and in society. The anger and disillusionment which have followed disclosure of the various scandals have no doubt taken their toll on church attendance and on people's readiness to listen to the church's leaders when moral issues are addressed. No doubt also we have been influenced by the secularising impetus which seems endemic in postmodern Western culture. And the internal tensions and polarisations which have latterly marked the Catholic Church generally can be found in Ireland too. The challenge to the church and its leadership, in terms of effective witness to and proclamation of the gospel, is complex and daunting.

Liam Ryan has proposed that, as regards the relationship between the church and society in the future, the role of the church might be that of con-science of society.[17] This idea was taken up by Enda McDonagh who, whilst granting its merit, raised some questions; 'Is the church the only conscience of society? Who as church shall speak for the conscience of society? Is this a task for the bishops only, or bishops and priests, or the laity. Is it an ecu-menical task for the churches working together, or one for the Catholic Church only? On what issues shall this conscience be voiced, on the tradi-tional issues of sexual morality, respect for life in terms of abortion or political violence, on education, or is there a whole wider range of issues? How are these issues discerned? How are conscience judgments formed about them? Who shall listen to this conscience? How shall its judgment be offered or imposed?'[18]

Ryan's suggestion and McDonagh's questions are perhaps even more apt now than when first made, and they intimate the complexity of the church's task. The questions are a good description of the agenda which must be tack-led by church leaderships which wish to influence Irish society as it seeks to articulate a value system for the times ahead. Some, of course, will want to say that these questions belong to the past, that the churches as institutions have lost their footing irretrievably. How can someone be 'a conscience' until his own house is put in order? Trust lost is painfully difficult to regain, when it can be regained at all.

---

17. 'The Church in Politics', *The Furrow* 30 (1979), no 1, p 17.
18. Enda McDonagh, *The Making of Disciples,* Dublin 1982, p 177.

Yet there are, as I said earlier, advantages and opportunities in the situation which has emerged in Ireland and, in terms of the church's self-understanding and its own spiritual and moral vision, there are some specific advantages and opportunities. We are in a time of fresh insight into the gospel truth that the Son of Man came not to be served but to serve.[19] It is a time of insight, too, into the truth that 'My kingdom is not from this world'.[20] There is a challenge to a deeper understanding of the injunction of Jesus, 'Do this in remembrance of me.'[21] It is possible to hope for a renewal of the church as institution, not only in aid of the faith and hope of its own membership, but also the better to fit it for its gospel call to be a leaven in society and a light in the world.

---

19. Mk 10:45.
20. Jn 18:36.
21. Lk 22:19.

Reconstructing Faith
for a New Century and a New Society

Dermot A. Lane

Ireland at the end of the twentieth century is undergoing unprecedented economic, social, political, cultural, and religious change. This change is having a dramatic effect on the quality of life throughout the length and breadth of the country. No human being, no parish or community, no institution is immune. A new Ireland is coming into being and this is something that must be welcomed. It is an Ireland that is more confident and competitive, more tolerant and plural, more connected to Europe and more open to the rest of the world. Enormous advances have taken place in education, healthcare, the arts, music, industry, information and communications technologies.

In the midst of all these changes a serious crisis exists, particularly within the Catholic Church. This crisis is more than an institutional crisis; it is a crisis affecting the very matrix and fabric of Christian faith itself.

The purpose of this reflection, coming at the end of a series of reflections on what is happening in modern Ireland on the eve of a new millennium, is to focus on the state of faith. We will begin by trying to describe what is happening to faith in the life of the Catholic Church at the turn of the century. From there, we will situate the erosion of faith within the larger European context of the enlightenment. Against that background, the possibility of reconstructing faith for the twenty-first century will be explored. By way of conclusion, we will show how a reconstructed faith needs the support of a new religious imagination.

I THE STATE OF CHRISTIAN FAITH AT THE END OF THE SECOND MILLENNIUM

Numerous surveys have been undertaken in recent years documenting the decline of the Catholic Church in the 1990s. They have described a significant fall in church attendance at Mass, a sharp decline in vocations to the priesthood and religious life, a diminishing credibility and relevance of moral and doctrinal teaching, and a distinct absence of planning and vision for the future. These phenomena are often attributed to a series of scandals within the church ranging from sexual abuse and other immoral behaviour to a lack of institutional transparency within the public domain by the leadership of the church. While these inexcusable and reprehensible realities have indeed damaged the image and life of the Catholic Church, there is more to the current crisis than sin and failure.

It would be wrong to imply that nothing positive is happening in the Catholic Church on the eve of a new millennium. There are new shoots of Christian life coming forth that deserve as much attention as the present crisis. These new beacons of hope include the existence of large numbers of men and women studying theology and religious education around the country, a programme of Pastoral Development and Renewal originating in the Dublin diocese and extending to other dioceses, the prophetic activities of the justice desk of the Conference of Religious of Ireland (CORI), and the existence of a vibrant post-primary Religion Teachers' Association. However, the focus of this reflection is on the existing crisis within the church.

A number of helpful analyses of the present crisis go beyond blaming recent scandals in the life of the church. Enda McDonagh talks tellingly about the church living through 'a dark and fragmentary time' and highlights the existence of so much estrangement and exclusion within the life of the church.[1] McDonagh rightly notes that these realities of course are not peculiar to the Catholic Church; they can be found throughout contemporary Irish society.

Michael Paul Gallagher claims that what is happening is 'a crisis not of creed but of culture, not of faith in itself but of the capacity to believe beyond ourselves'.[2] Gallagher is surely correct in his diagnosis of a crisis of culture and our capacity to believe beyond ourselves. Once this is conceded, however, you do in fact have a crisis of faith, which is the real issue facing church and society in Ireland at the end of the twentieth century.

Seamus Ryan has likened the clerical church in Ireland to that of an overgrown pot-bound plant which is beginning to choke itself by its own roots because they have nowhere to go. The roots of the church are yearning to break out and to find a new ambience in which to grow – but they are too fearful.[3]

Another image used by some to describe what is happening in the Irish church is that of a boxer in a ring who has been knocked out but continues to go through the boxing motions out of memory. This image is helpful because it captures one of the central elements in the current crisis, namely that the institutional church is in danger of promoting the dead faith of the living as distinct from the living faith of the dead. Handing on the content of the faith without attending to the personal act of faith can give the illusion that all is well in the present. If the content and practice of the faith

1. Enda McDonagh, *Faith in Fragments*, Dublin: The Columba Press, 1996.
2. Michael P. Gallagher, 'From Social to Cultural Secularization', *Louvain Studies*, Summer 1999, pp 103-118 at 104
3. Seamus Ryan, 'Are We busy about the Right things?', *The Church in a New Ireland*, edited by S. Mac Réamoinn, Dublin: The Columba Press, 1996, pp 69-83 at 81.

remains the same while the foundations informing that content have shifted, then a serious tension arises within the life of faith. There is increasing pastoral and theological evidence of the presence of this tension within the lives of people, especially when they are faced with hard choices, personal crisis, human tragedy and death.

It is the view of many today that the foundations of faith have been shaken by the current crisis of culture within the western world and that until closer attention is given to these shifts then the communication of the content of faith will be only skin deep. This crisis of culture derives from such factors as the ambiguous legacy of the eighteenth-century enlightenment, the contemporary reaction to the enlightenment, the pervasive presence of value-free media, the revolution in communications and information technology, and the increasing presence of a mass culture through the process of globalisation. We will confine ourselves here to the influence of the enlightenment.

The enlightenment, often called the Age of Reason, unfolded through Europe over the last two hundred years with significant side effects on Christianity and in particular Christian faith. A once thoroughly Christian Europe has become, over a period of around one hundred years, a thoroughly secularised and now secularist Europe. This change in Europe of course took place gradually over a period of time. However, what has happened in Europe over two hundred years is now happening in Ireland within a period, roughly speaking, of twenty years since the papal visit of 1979. In Ireland the impact of the enlightenment has been telescoped into about twenty years of dramatic social, political, economic, and cultural change.

In the late nineteenth century Ireland was concerned about survival from the famine, whereas in the twentieth century the emphasis was placed on links between nationalism and Catholicism. In the last few decades, however, the ethos of enlightenment has taken a grip and hold in Ireland like never before. It is this new-found freedom, inspired by the spirit of the enlightenment with its promise of endless progress and personal fulfilment, that lies behind the present crisis of faith in the Catholic Church. To be sure scandals have played a part in the decline of faith – but far more influential has been the late arrival in Ireland of the enlightenment. Scandals in the church paved the way for an uncritical adoption of the philosophy of the Enlightenment in contemporary Ireland. The enlightenment, however, is a highly ambiguous reality carrying within itself seeds of life and destruction at one and the same time.

II THE ENLIGHTENMENT AND ITS IMPACT ON IRELAND

In discussing the enlightenment it needs to be noted immediately that the European enlightenment was by no means a single movement. Instead the

European enlightenment was an amalgam of different philosophical movements ranging from scepticism to empiricism to positivism to a cold rationalism. In spite of this variety, there are common themes. These include the primacy of reason over tradition, authority and religion. The enlightenment heralded an era of independent, autonomous and disengaged reason. Further, the spirit of the enlightenment sought to promote liberty, equality and fraternity, or as we might say today, freedom, justice and individual rights. In addition, enlightenment stood for progress, human emancipation from superstition, and the promise of personal fulfilment. Lastly, the enlightenment set out to tame nature and to bring an end to pain and suffering. There can be little doubt that the enlightenment has brought enormous benefits to humankind, especially in terms of modern medicine, science and technology.

However, there is a price to be paid for the progress brought about by the enlightenment. Walter Benjamin pointed out over fifty years ago that every great work of civilisation is at the same time a work of barbarism. More and more people now agree that we must reckon with what Horkheimer and Adorno have called 'the dialectic of enlightenment', that is, the existence of a dark side to the enlightenment. Horkheimer and Adorno point out that 'the enlightenment has always aimed at liberating men from fear and establishing their sovereignty. Yet the fully enlightened earth radiates disaster triumphant.'[4]

Looking back over the European enlightenment of two hundred years, it has now become clear that its legacy is deeply ambiguous. A lot of what was once called progress now appears as regress, many so-called developments have brought underdevelopment, the claim of a detached rationality has been found to have its own particular agenda, and the idea of value-free science and research is itself value-laden. Examples of this ambiguity abound in terms of the damage done to the environment, the harmful interference with the natural food chain, the traffic congestion of modern cities and the continuing gap between rich and poor within modern, market driven economies.

It would be historically inaccurate to hold that the enlightenment set out to deconstruct religion and faith – though it did seek to purge faith of what it called myth, superstition and projection. That the Christian faith was in need of criticism and reform few would deny. However in doing this, the enlightenment had the effect unintentionally of privatising faith. Probably the most serious effect of the enlightenment on faith has been the reduction of the mystery of God to the level of just one more item of information alongside other pieces of information, and just one more explanation for the

---

4. M. Horkheimer and T. W. Adorno, *Dialectic of the Enlightenment,* New York: Continuum, 1972, p 3.

existence of the world alongside other explanations. In response to the enlightenment, faith itself unwittingly became influenced with enlightenment suppositions. Christian faith lost contact with the historical tradition of Christian revelation and allowed itself to become a largely rationalist construct alongside other systems.

Given these observations it is important that the Irish enlightenment should not repeat the mistakes of the European enlightenment, though all the signs suggest that this is what is happening today. Can the Irish enlightenment learn from the exaggerations of the European enlightenment in its absolute critique of authority, tradition and religion?

For example, is it possible, indeed is it desirable, to abandon all reference to tradition and history in seeking to forge a new national, European, and international identity? To be sure there were serious mistakes made and extraordinary levels of corruption existed within institutions in the past. Many will point to the mounting evidence from recent enquiries and tribunals to justify the treatment of all institutions with suspicion. Can we live only with and out of suspicion? Is it possible to reconstruct the present *de novo* without reference to the past? It will be argued that those who do not know the past are bound to repeat it. Can we have hope in the future without memories, positive and negative, from the past?

Allowing for this underlying ambiguity within the enlightenment project there is now beginning to emerge a desire by some to abandon altogether the modern project. This desire is expressed in the rise of a post-modern sensibility. Post-modernism is more a mood than a movement, more a reaction than a clear reconstruction, more a protest than a concrete proposal about the future. The term 'post-modern' is extremely vague and has come to acquire too many different meanings too quickly. Nevertheless, post-modernism does capture a sense of deep dissatisfaction with the modern world. Post-modernism, or post-enlightenment as some like to call it, is about deconstructing the meta-narratives of the modern world, decentring the absolute position of the human subject, and destabilising all systems in favour of particularity, pluralism and otherness. In its extreme form, post-modernism gives rise to excessive fragmentation, produces relativism, and can lead to a despairing nihilism. In its favour, however, post-modernism has drawn attention to the neglected value and significance of difference, otherness and plurality.

There are at present three different types of post-modernism: radical post-modernism, nostalgic post-modernism and counter-post-modernism. Radical post-modernism takes a historicist perspective on the whole of life. It rejects the idea of universal reason, suggesting that it is an illusion belonging to the dominant group in society. This particular post-modernism also calls into question the reality of human nature and subjectivity, implying that the self is simply the outcome of particular relationships of power and desire. Radical post-modernism holds that history is merely something made up as we go along without any underlying continuities.

At the other extreme there is nostalgic post-modernism which harks back to the supposed securities and certainties of the classical era. Between these two polarities, there is the middle position of counter-post-modernism which sees the modern project as unfinished, in need of further refinement and development. These 'late moderns' suggest that modernity is something that can be corrected through attention to dialogue, hermeneutics, narrative, communicative reason and ethics.

It is against this background that Ireland in the late twentieth century finds itself at a strange crossroads. On the one hand it seeks to adopt the European enlightenment at a time when many in the West are having serious reservations about the liberal enlightenment project of modernity as a way of life. On the other hand, the alternative of a radical post-modern sensibility offers an empty prospect. Is it possible to seek a way forward that retains what is best in the enlightenment impulse while being aware of its underlying ambiguity and at the same time adopting some of the positive aspects of the post-modern mood? There are those in Ireland today who would like to go back to a pre-modern period as if the enlightenment had never happened, especially in areas of faith and morality. Equally there are those in Ireland at the close of the century who wish to adopt uncritically the spirit of enlightenment without qualification or any awareness of its dark side. A good example can be found in a current advertisement seeking funds for the Third World which proudly declares that it is 'non-denominational and non-political' in the name of an autonomous reason. It would be interesting to know how a body calling itself non-denominational and non-political could address the problems of the Third World!

Whether we like it or not we are all children of the enlightenment and it is within the broad horizons of the enlightenment that we can and must understand the world around us. It is only in virtue of the enlightenment itself that we can offer constructive criticism and corrections of the enlightenment project of modernity. To this extent the crisis of faith that has become part of modern Ireland can only be addressed within the crucible of an enlightenment-modern-framework.

III TOWARDS AN ENLIGHTENED FAITH FOR A NEW CENTURY

Given the advent of the enlightenment in Ireland, and the prospect of a creeping radical post-modernity, what future does Christian faith have? Can the Christian faith succeed within this doubly ambiguous situation? At the close of the twentieth century, Christian faith is caught in a highly precarious position: sidelined by the successes of the Celtic Tiger as a symbolic expression of the enlightenment values and threatened by extinction from the nihilism of a radical post-modernity. Faced with these two possibilities the obvious temptation for faith is either to retreat into pre-modern forms or to brazen out the storm of the enlightenment by adhering in a fundamentalist way to the existing propositions of the content of faith.

There is evidence of some yielding to one or other of these temptations within contemporary Ireland. Such temptations should be resisted for various reasons. First of all, a faith that ignores the enlightenment, especially the emerging chastened version of the enlightenment, is no longer 'faith' or 'Christian'. Faith without contact with reason is not faith but a distortion of faith such as fideism. Further, a faith that does not interact with the surrounding culture is hardly a living faith, nor is it truly Christian since the centre of Christianity is rooted in historical interaction with culture. Lastly, a faith that takes refuge in the past is ultimately a faith without hope in the future. Instead, therefore, of pulling down the blinds on faith, what is required at this moment in Ireland is the courage to open up a new dialogue between faith and reason, knowledge and belief, culture and religion, church and society.

In opening up this dialogue between faith and life it will be necessary to overcome a number of misunderstandings that have arisen from the prevailing influence of the enlightenment itself. These include the privatisation of faith or the removal of faith from public debate, the supposed non-rationality or lack of plausibility that is perceived to attach to faith, the impression that faith is extrinsic to human knowing, that is, some kind of add-on or extra to human reason, and that the activity of faith is somehow or other the peculiar property of religious people. To meet the challenge of the enlightenment and post-enlightenment and these particular misunderstandings surrounding faith today in modern Ireland, it will be necessary to rediscover faith as something intrinsic to the human condition, to recover an apologetical element as essential to faith in a secular age, and to retrieve the lost unity between faith and reason.

a. Faith is intrinsic to human existence.
For too long, and especially under the influence of the enlightenment, the impression was often given that faith is something only religious people have and that by making faith rare and exclusive to one group of people it was making it all the more valuable. In truth, however, the opposite is the case. Faith is a universal phenomenon and as such is constitutive of the human condition. Without faith in the value of life and the meaningfulness of exist-

ence, it would be impossible to promote human flourishing. In a very important sense it is faith that makes the world go around and spins the global village.
Everybody lives out of faith, including unbelievers, agnostics and atheists. The
kind of faith in question here is often called basic or primordial or human faith;
it is that trust in life and acceptance of people which is pre-supposed as the necessary condition of all human thinking, talking and doing. This underlying
basic faith assumes that life makes sense and is worth living, that life is of value
in spite of the presence of suffering and death, loneliness and doubt, injustice
and oppression. In an important sense this basic, primordial faith is a way of
structuring life and organising the multiplicity of human experiences and activities that take place in life.

Not everyone seeks to justify or examine or ground this common primordial
faith in the meaningfulness of life and the worthwhileness of existence. The
role of religion, more specifically of theology, is to offer an ultimate ground
and absolute source for such meaning and values. It is this final ground and
source that justifies basic faith. Faith in God explicates the existence of basic
primordial faith. For many the basis of primordial faith goes no further than
this world, whereas the basis of religious faith embraces this world and, at the
same time, a transcendent source. A close relationship, therefore, as well as a
distinction, exists between basic faith and religious faith. Yet the object of
basic faith and religious faith is different, the former being finite and historical and the latter being infinite and transcendent. This emphasis on faith as
universal and intrinsic to the human condition highlights an old but forgotten New Testament truth: you cannot have faith in God without also having
faith in humanity. (1 Jn 4:16-21)

b. An apologetical element within Christian faith.
Although most of the fathers of the enlightenment were believers, the logical
outcome of their work has been a radical form of secularism. This secularism
of enlightenment rationality has infiltrated our understanding of nature,
history and culture. For example, the disenchantment of nature, the removal
of providence from history, and the elimination of religion from culture has
had a profound effect on the way we look at life, society and the world today.
Consequently statements of faith cannot take for granted the existence of
God, the reality of revelation or the authority of the church. To begin a statement by claiming that 'the bible says' or 'the church teaches' or 'the Pope/the
bishops affirm' is to beg a host of questions about revelation, the normativity
of Christianity and the role of a teaching authority that can no longer be
taken as self-evident.

The point of departure for statements of faith must be shared human
experience, the promotion of human and ecological values, a concern for justice

in society and the earth community. Only from within this experiential human and ecological context will religious faith begin to get a hearing and to make sense. The real value of an apologetical theology is that it keeps open the dialogue between faith and the world. It is important in a secular age that the person of faith be able to speak, not just the language of Christian tradition but also the language of the world in which that tradition is to be represented. If this can happen, then Christian faith will be enriched by the wisdom of the secular world and the secular world will be challenged by Christian faith.

In other words, the intellectual credibility and plausibility of faith must be argued for and not simply taken for granted. The call in modern Ireland for greater openness, transparency and accountability within politics must also be applied analogously to statements of faith by Christians in the future. A Christian faith that is accountable to 'the other' and before the world is a faith that will be taken seriously. In the words of the New Testament, we must always be ready to give an account of the hope that is within each one of us. (1 Pet 3:15) In this sense, Christian faith in the twenty-first century will require a strong apologetical element within its narrative.

c. Recovering the unity of faith and reason
One of the most serious side-effects of the enlightenment in general has been the separation of faith from reason. This separation in turn has resulted in the isolation and privatisation of faith. The sidelining of faith within public debate is increasingly evident in Ireland in the 1990s, with the exception of the Justice Desk of CORI. It is remarkable that the cultural renaissance taking place in Ireland in the last decade of this century in the arts, literature, poetry and music is devoid of any explicit Christian impulse. There is growing unease, and sometimes even alienation, among many intellectuals with the Christian reality in Ireland today. It is assumed that faith and reason are in conflict and this assumption affects areas as diverse as the dialogue that should take place between religion and culture, faith and literature, ethics and economics, religion and science, law and morality.

There are various reasons for this divorce between faith and reason in contemporary Ireland. These include factors such as the relative absence of theology in the universities, a preoccupation with orthodoxy by the institutional church, an absence of open and honest debate within church circles on controversial issues, and the neglect of a legitimate pluralism within the unity of Christian faith itself. As a result, statements of faith are more often than not treated with a hermeneutics of deep suspicion. It only compounds the problem for church people to blame the media or to suggest that some are out to get the church. Most people, the vast majority of people in Ireland, are principally interested in discovering the truth about the big questions in life concerning life and death, brokenness and healing, history and eternity, suffering, evil and God. The church does have an important faith perspective on questions of this kind but unfortunately it appears reluctant to enter into debate.

A church that once upon a time thought that it had all the answers to the big questions of life now finds it difficult to admit that it does not have the answers, and even more difficult to journey humbly and honestly with others in search of light and truth. This is all the more remarkable for a community which declares that it lives by faith. If we acknowledge that the life of faith, the personal act of Christian faith, embraces light and darkness, joy and sadness, emptiness and fullness, absence and presence, loneliness and communion, certainty and doubt, ecstasy and dryness, then there is no reason why the Christian community cannot journey with others of goodwill in a shared search for truth. The life of faith, of Christian faith in particular, is as much about being able to ask the big questions of life and being able to live with ambiguities as it is about having answers to the troubling issues of existence

One way forward out of this marginalisation of Christian faith within modern Ireland is to recover the classical unity between faith and reason. In pre-Christian times, great philosophers like Aristotle argued for a dynamic interplay between faith and reason in arriving at progress within human understanding and knowledge. This unity of faith and reason was continued and developed within the Christian tradition by people like Augustine and Aquinas who claimed it was necessary to believe in order to understand and equally necessary to reason rigorously in order to have faith. Faith and reason have been critical but constructive companions in the progress of human thought right up to the time of the enlightenment. Indeed, ironically and paradoxically, it was in virtue of this unity between faith and reason that the enlightenment came into being. Since the enlightenment, however, there has been the gradual separation of faith and reason. This separation has resulted in the emergence of an uncritical, passive faith bordering on fideism and an inflated, self-sufficient perception of reason amounting to rationalism. On the eve of a new millennium there is too much fideism and rationalism within contemporary Ireland and insufficient dialogue between faith and reason.

In emphasising the unity between faith and reason, it is important, however, not to reduce faith to reason or reason to faith. Faith is not about proving the existence of God or demonstrating that God offers the best possible explanation for the existence of the world. Instead faith is a venture, a personal response to the presence and absence of God revealed in human experience, in the history of Judaism, in the life of Jesus, and other religions within the context of the gift of creation and the wonder of human creativity. This personal response embraces elements of trust, self-surrender and love.

The personal response of the individual to the revelation of God is not something that can be coerced or forced; rather it is always a free response enabled by community to the grace of existence itself. Further, the *intelligibility* of this response is available principally *within the experience* of actually responding in faith, and not something prior to the act of faith. In addition it must be noted that the act of faith does not demand or require that one subscribe to claims that contradict the established findings of reason because, ultimately speaking, faith and reason compliment rather than contradict each other. In maintaining this unity between faith and reason, faith will prompt reason to expand its horizons beyond a merely instrumental view of rationality to embrace the more enduring questions about the search for meaning, truth and wisdom.

IV. IN SEARCH OF A NEW IMAGINATION FOR FAITH
IN THE TWENTY-FIRST CENTURY

Allowing for the possibility of reconstructing Christian faith along the lines indicated, it should be acknowledged that there are new pressure points on Christian faith that must be faced. One way of dealing with these new pressures on Christian faith is in and through a reconfiguration of the religious imagination. A little like the paradigm changes that have taken place in science over the centuries, a somewhat similar paradigm shift is required of theology on the eve of the new millennium. This shift is likened by many to the imaginative change that took place in the second century in the movement from Jewish Christianity to Hellenistic Christianity. Paradigm shifts, or changes in the configuration of the human imagination, do not take place overnight. Instead they occur when a particular constellation of changes and values, beliefs and cultural shifts begins to coalesce into a new picture, a new way of looking at life and interpreting experience that is more fruitful and productive.

What are the pressure points suggesting this shift in the way Christian faith conceives and imagines itself? These new challenges to Christian faith can be divided into intra-theological pressure points and extra-theological challenges.

Within theology itself one of the most serious challenges facing faith is the existence of so much apathy. The burning issue within Christian conversation at the end of the twentieth century in Ireland is no longer unbelief but religious indifference, summed up in the observation that 'God is missing but not missed'. Apathy concerning religion abounds in modern Ireland and poses a most serious challenge to faith and theology. An apathetic theology generates an apathetic people. Anyone who seeks to talk about the Christian faith must be prepared to cope with 'the yawn factor' among the audience.

This new phenomenon, 'the yawn factor', is particularly evident among the younger generation and represents one of the most telling critiques of faith in modern Ireland. It is a signal for those who have eyes to see, to recognise the apparent flatness attaching to the Christian message, or what David Tracy refers to as the deadening uniformity of the univocal mind in so much theological discourse.[5] Christian concepts have lost the hold, fascination and urgency they once had. This does not mean that the compelling message of Jesus about the coming Reign of God, or the preaching of the early church about the crucified and risen Christ present in the Spirit, is any the less relevant or important today; it does mean however that the images and concepts used in communicating the good news have become flat. The issue of so much apathy and indifference today about the Christian message is ultimately a question about the imagination. The existence of so much 'yawn' is itself a demand for a new imagination out of which the Christian story might be retold. It is instructive to note that Mary Warnock associates the loss of imagination with a certain 'joylessness' about the world in which we live.[6] Such 'joylessness' is another way of describing the presence of apathy and indifference *vis à vis* Christian faith today.

A second pressure point on Christian faith comes from the ecumenical movement. The teaching of the Second Vatican Council on ecumenism and the very significant number of agreed statements among different Christian churches (such as ARCIC and the joint declaration by the Catholic Church and the Lutheran World Federation on the Doctrine of Justification signed in October 1999) raise serious questions about the lack of progress towards some form of visible unity among the Christian churches. The strong reaction 'from below', to the publication of *One Bread, One Body* (1998) 'from above', among so many people in Ireland was itself a heartfelt cry against the present wintry season in ecumenical relations. The failure of the churches to draw closer together is a failure ultimately of the imagination, that is a failure within the Catholic and Protestant imagination to unify and integrate what appears to be separate and different. This failure by the churches in Ireland to move forward in a visible way is now contrasted in a particularly poignant way by the success, however fragile, of politicians of the North and South who were able to come together to sign the Good Friday Peace Agreement in 1998.

A third intra-theological pressure point on Christian faith is its apparent inability to relate to the other major religions of the world. The positive eval-

---

5. David Tracy, *The Analogical Imagination: Christian Theology and Culture of Pluralism*, New York: Crossroad, 1981, p 413.
6. Mary Warnock, 'Religious Imagination', *Religious Imagination*, edited by James P. Mackey, Edinburgh: Edinburgh University Press, 1986, pp 142-157 at 147.

uation of world religions by the Second Vatican Council (1965) and the World Council of Churches (1979) challenges the faith of all Christians to move from a position of imperial exclusivity to open inclusivity in relation to the other religions of the world. If, as Vatican II, teaches the non-Christian religions contain 'rays of that faith which illumines all humankind', 'elements of truth and Grace', and 'seeds of the Word', then Christian faith can no longer remain indifferent to the presence of the other religions. The challenge to enter into a real dialogue with others should not be seen as a threat to Christian identity but a unique opportunity to intensify and deepen Christian self-understanding. If the Christian symbols have become dulled through the passage of time, then there can be little doubt that they will acquire a new vibrancy through the encounter with other religions, especially the monotheistic religions of Judaism and Islam which have a common origin with Christianity in the faith of Abraham. Once again, if this encounter with the other religions is to take place, it will require a new kind of Christian imagination.

Similar pressure points having a bearing on faith can be found from extra-theological sources. These particular pressure points derive from developments taking place outside the Christian tradition within the broad stream of culture. If it is true to say that one of the distinctive features of Christian faith is that it has one foot planted in tradition and the other in the world, then these pressure points are equally important for the life of faith. Only a sample of such pressure points can be offered here.

The first among these is the emergence of a new global and cosmic consciousness. Through the information and communications revolution the world has become a global village like never before. And yet at the same time we have come to realise that the size of the universe, that is the cosmos, is far more vast and complex than we ever imagined up to now. The emergence of a new cosmic story about the origins and evolutionary development of planet-earth over a period of fifteen thousand million years is an important element in this new consciousness. Coupled with this, we have come to realise that planet-earth is a grain of sand within a vast galaxy which is itself just one among a possible fifty billion galaxies.

A second pressure point in faith comes from a post-modern consciousness which gives a new valuation to difference, otherness and diversity. This new emphasis helps us to realise that diversity is an intrinsic part of life and as such has an enormous potential to be a source of enrichment rather than division.

A third pressure point, coming from science, helps us to realise that everything in the world is organically inter-related, inter-connected, inter-dependent and at the same time extremely fragile, uncertain and unpredictable.

This particular awareness increases the urgency of devising a new global ethic and corporate responsibility for the survival of the earth in the third millennium.

The weaving together of these insights into a meaningful picture requires a new imagination, a new way of picturing the world in which we live. The world of discrete, autonomous and independent entities, as put forward by the enlightenment for example, is no longer a viable world. There is a clear need to imagine the world, and ourselves within the world, in a new way. From the point of view of Christian faith, this amounts to a call for a new religious imagination.

The human faculty of imagination is one of the most neglected and most misunderstood areas within contemporary theology, in spite of significant work by William Lynch, David Tracy and James P. Mackey. The human imagination is a kind of 'sorting office' or 'template' within the mind that gathers, organises and unifies a great variety of images of life into a meaningful whole. Imagination has the capacity to integrate the buzzing and booming multiplicity of particular human experiences into a universal framework that holds them together in a way that makes sense. The human imagination is, as it were, 'a bridge' between human experience, understanding and interpretation. It is the imagination that enables human understanding to take place and it is impossible for understanding to exist without the power of the imagination. Not only children but also adults all the time live out of their imagination. The difference between the imagination of the child and the imagination of the adult is that children move with great ease from one imaginative construction to another, whereas adults tend to get fixed within one imaginative framework. It is artists, poets, and literary people above all who help us to move out from one particular configuration of the imagination to another. Most of all it is the human imagination that enables people to picture new possibilities, to unify what appears to be separate, to hold together light and darkness in the one place, and to envisage a future with hope.

If the faculty of imagination can enable us to do this, then it will be possible for Christian faith within the ecumenical movement to affirm a new unity within diversity and within interfaith dialogue to discover similarities within differences. For Christian faith to be true to itself in the next century it will, therefore, be necessary to be ecumenical and inter-religious without losing its own particular identity. This will mean that Christian faith will have to learn to embrace difference, otherness and diversity and know that in doing so it will be able to intensify and deepen its own self-understanding.

This call for a new religious imagination is not something that is foreign to the Christian tradition. Instead it is something that happened at the very foundations of Christianity in the encounter between Jesus and Judaism, and subsequently in the process of inculturation that took place in the second century as Christian faith moved into the new Hellenistic world. Later on, there was the development of the analogical imagination in the middle ages and, subsequent to that, the emergence of the dialectical imagination at the time of the Reformation. On the eve of the third millennium it is not only possible but necessary for Christianity to undergo a similar but different reconfiguration of the imagination in expressing the good news brought by Jesus.

In brief, Christian faith in the new century and new society of Ireland will have to present itself as intrinsic to the human condition and not outside it, as apologetical and not authoritarian, as ecumenical and not sectarian, as inter-religious and not exclusive, as affectively reasonable and not coldly rational. Such qualities and characteristics of Christian faith are an intrinsic part of the dynamism of the mystery of Jesus Christ as the eternal Word and Wisdom of God made flesh in history.[7]

7. I am grateful to Elizabeth Lovatt-Dolan and Terence W. Tilley for helpful comments on a draft of this text.

The Contributors

BRUCE ARNOLD is Literary Editor of the *Irish Independent,* and the author of a number of books which include biographies of politicians, writers and artists. He has written widely on ethics in politics, with an emphasis on the moral obligations of politicians, the responsibilities of those who elect them to power, and the constitutional requirements which are imposed on the people and on the institutions of state.

DENIS CARROLL teaches theology in the School of Hebrew, Biblical and Theological Studies at Dublin University. He has written a number of books on Irish history and theology. His most recent publications include *Land: Christian Perspectives on Development Issues* (1998) and *Unusual Suspects: Twelve Radical Clergy* (1998).

MICHAEL DRUMM is lecturer in theology at Mater Dei Institute of Education, Dublin. He is author of *Passage to Pasch* (1998), *Famine: Christian Perspectives on Development Issues* (1998), and co-author of *A Sacramental People, Volume 1: Initiation* (1999).

GARRET FITZGERALD is a former Irish Foreign Minister and Taoiseach who had earlier careers in air transport, academic life, and economic consultancy, and who is now a journalist and lecturer, with a particular interest in Irish demography and social issues.

TOM GIBLIN is a Jesuit, living in Cherry Orchard and working as a graduate fellow in the Economics Department in University College Dublin, while completing a Ph.D in economics. He also works in the Jesuit Centre for Faith and Justice.

PATRICK HANNON is Professor of Moral Theology and Director of Post-graduate Studies at St Patrick's College, Maynooth. Author of *Church, State, Morality and Law,* (Dublin: Gill and Macmillan, 1992), and various articles on religion, morality and law, and on human rights.

LINDA HOGAN is a graduate of St Patrick's College, Maynooth and Trinity College Dublin, where she gained her Ph.D in 1993. She holds the post of Lecturer in Gender, Ethics and Religion at the University of Leeds. She is the author of *From Women's Experience to Feminist Theology,* (Sheffield Academic Press, 1995).

JOHN HORGAN is Professor of Journalism at Dublin City University. He is a frequent contributor to newspapers and other publications in Ireland and abroad on a range of professional, academic and political topics. He is the author of a number of books, most recently including biographies of Sean Lemass and Mary Robinson.

DERMOT A. LANE is President of Mater Dei Institute of Education and Parish Priest of Balally in Dublin 16. His most recent publication is *Keeping Hope Alive: Stirrings in Christian Theology* (1996).

ANNE LOONEY is a graduate of Mater Dei Institute, and taught Religious Education in a Dublin secondary school for thirteen years. She is currently seconded to the National Council for Curriculum and Assessment. She is pursuing doctoral studies in curriculum policy at the Institute of Education of the University of London.

AIDAN MATHEWS is a writer whose work includes *Lipstick on the Host* (fiction) and *According to the Small Hours* (poetry).

SEAN MCDONAGH is a Columban Missionary. He is co-ordinator of the Justice, Peace and Integrity of Creation Ministry for Columban Missionaries. His most recent publication is *Passion for the Earth* (1995).

GERRY O'HANLON SJ is a former Lecturer in Systematic Theology and Dean of Theology at the Milltown Institute of Theology and Philosophy. He has served as a member of the Department of Theological Questions of the Irish Inter-Church Meeting. He is currently Provincial of the Society of Jesus in Ireland.

ANDREW PIERCE is lecturer in church history and theology at the Church of Ireland Theological College in Dublin. He also lectures in Trinity College Dublin and at the Irish School of Ecumenics. His research interests focus on the appeal to experience in modern theology.

MARY SUTTON studied Economics in Ireland and Canada. She worked for the Irish Commission for Justice and Peace and the Overseas Development Institute (London) before joining Trócaire in 1982, where she is now the Head of the Communications and Education Department.